MAKING THE SCENE: NASHVILLE

How to Live, Network, and Succeed in Music City

LIAM SULLIVAN

Hal Leonard Books
An Imprint of Hal Leonard Corporation

Published in 2012 by Hal Leonard Books
An Imprint of Hal Leonard Corporation
7777 West Bluemound Road
Milwaukee, WI 53213

Trade Book Division Editorial Offices
33 Plymouth St., Montclair, NJ 07042

All photographs by Liam Sullivan
Nashville map from Shutterstock.com

Printed in the United States of America

Book design by Adam Fulrath

Library of Congress Cataloging-in-Publication Data
Sullivan, Liam Napier, 1966-
Making the scene : Nashville : How to live, network, and succeed in Music City / Liam Sullivan.
     pages cm
1. Music trade--Tennessee--Nashville--Vocational guidance. 2. Country music--Tennessee--Nashville--Vocational guidance. 3. Country music--Tennessee--Nashville--History and criticism. 4. Nashville (Tenn.)--Guidebooks. 5. Nashville (Tenn.)--Directories. I. Title.
ML3790.S79 2012
781.642023'76855--dc23
                          2012025306

ISBN 978-1-6177-4089-3

www.halleonardbooks.com

MAKING THE SCENE: NASHVILLE

This book is for my mom and dad
and to their boundless encouragement
of my passion for music and travel over the years.

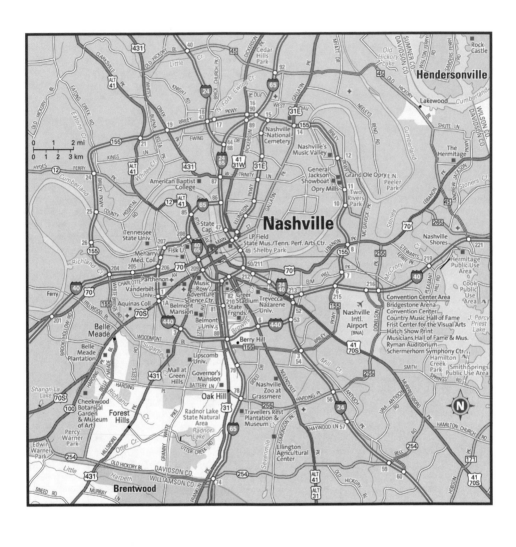

CONTENTS

ACKNOWLEDGMENTS

A special thanks is in order to the following:

John Cerullo, Matt Cerullo, Polly Watson, and the entire team at Hal Leonard, Tracey Howerton and the entire staff at the Nashville Public Library, Dr. Don Cusic, Ronnie Pugh, Ralph Murphy, Sheree Spoltore, Debi Champion, Amber Hayes, Ryan Michaels, Patti Donahoe, Mark Lonsway, Kirsti Manna, Julie Forester, Dr. John Rumble, Bradley Collins, Phoebe Blume, Mark Weiss, Vincent Abbate, Patrick Hemsworth, Emile Menasche, Chris Soldo, Tootsies Orchid Lounge, Robert's Western World, Tim "Fred" Godwin, Jeff Epstein, Dan "Dino" Zaccari, Robert Ellis Orrall, Tim Fink, Joe Limardi, Eddie Stubbs, Bill Cody and Charlie Mattos at WSM 650 AM radio, Amy Kurland, Julie Roberts, Jeff King, Steve Komen, and Hank Locklin Jr. Finally, thanks to my family, friends, and the good people of Nashville who have taught me that wherever there is music there is always a way into the light. Rock On!

INTRODUCTION

66 I've never known a musician who regretted being one. Whatever deceptions life may have in store for you, music itself is not going to let you down.99—Virgil Thompson

Nashville, Tennessee. The name is known around the world as the home of country music. It has been referenced in hundreds of songs and if you say, "Nashville, Tennessee," out loud long enough, you'll notice it has a musical ring all its own. The warmth of those two words has drawn musicians of all stripes to this city for decades. For Nashville's original inhabitants, playing music served as relief from the hard work and toil they endured forging a new life. They employed instruments such as violins (fiddles), guitars, and mandolins. They called out in song on back porches, churches, hilltops, valleys, and plateaus that make up the landscape of the state of Tennessee. It can be argued that music, to the early settlers, was as important to them as the food they put on their tables. Music was their spiritual nourishment. The songs they sang often drew upon themes from scripture, local folklore, and the hardships of working the land. They were songs of faith, everyday struggles, love, heartache, and pain. As country music grew in scope those themes would remain the bedrock from which future songwriters could pull inspiration.

Nashville is unquestionably a historic music hub. The Ryman Auditorium, which sits in the heart of downtown Nashville, has served as a beacon, if you will, for musicians for more than a hundred years. If you're a musician, you *want* to play the Ryman Auditorium. The longest-running radio show in American history, the *Grand Ole Opry*, still broadcasts live from the Ryman Auditorium a few times each month. Situated around the Ryman down on lower Broadway in Nashville are the honky-tonks: bars bustling with live music, tourists, locals, and musicians from around the world. There is no other place like it. Amateur and professional musicians flock to Nashville each year to become part of what has become a musician's paradise. However, the musical landscape has evolved beyond country music. Now, every genre of music is represented in Nashville: jazz, blues, rock, R&B, soul, country, and bluegrass. With the completion of the Schermerhorn Symphony Center in 2007, opera and classical music are represented as well.

Preparation Meets Opportunity

Moving to any new city is a challenge. For musicians, that challenge can sometimes be greater. As musicians, we make noise. There's no getting around it. We thrive on working with other musicians and either playing in rehearsal spaces or gigging out. We need spaces where we can create, record, and hang out with other musicians. As musicians, we also need to know where to play, where to buy gear, where to see live music, network, and exchange ideas. We need to know where to live, where to buy a car, where to buy clothing or that cool hat. We also need to find jobs that fit a musician's lifestyle.

As musicians, we prepare, we practice. We work at our craft so that when "preparation meets opportunity," we're ready. Therefore, moving to Nashville should be looked at in the same way. We need to set a budget and take care of all the variables before making that big move. Think of it as preparing for a gig. What will you need? A guitar tuner, an extra set of strings, extra pairs of drum sticks, batteries, a backup guitar, mics, patch cords, etc. In assembling these, you are prepared, not scrabbling around at the last minute asking other musicians in other bands at the gig, "Hey, can we borrow your drum stool? Our keyboard player needs something to sit on." As musicians, we are constantly learning, not only from the music we listen to, but from people who see us perform. In the coming chapters you will read firsthand advice from musicians who have moved to Nashville and the challenges that they faced. I'll also be interviewing music industry professionals who will offer up helpful tips so that once you get settled you can make your plan of attack and get your music heard.

There will be tips on how to get a music publishing deal and the benefits of becoming an ASCAP, BMI, or SESAC member. You'll read about networking at open mic/writers' nights, and how to find writing partners for co-writing projects. And finally, you'll learn the best approach to getting a gig so that you're not playing to the crickets on a Tuesday night at 1:00 A.M. I'll also offer up my own personal account of the challenges that I faced as a musician when I first moved to Nashville and describe some of the hurdles that I had to overcome in order to make Nashville my new home.

The Nitty-Gritty

The social diversity of this country is as vast as its borders. This should play a part in your thinking when relocating to Nashville. Social nuances vary greatly from the East to the West, North, and South. Nashville, like any city, has its own rhythm, and the more in tune you are to that rhythm, the better off you'll be. Therefore, I'll explain how Nashville became such an important music city, and how everyone from early music pioneers to today's country music legends helped make that happen. Once you've figured out the lay of the land you'll want to branch out to the various services that musicians rely on, as well as where to eat after a late-night gig (very important!). You'll need to know where to get CDs made and duplicated. You'll need to find local producers and recording studios so you can make a demo. Additionally, you'll need to make the most of contacting local social networking sites, newspapers, radio, and TV stations that will further help you promote your image and build a following. Understanding how this music town works before you arrive is vital. By supplying you with historical references, modern resources, and interviews with a wide range of music professionals, this book will help guide you through the challenges of moving to Music City USA, Nashville, Tennessee.

CHAPTER 1
Welcome to Nashville

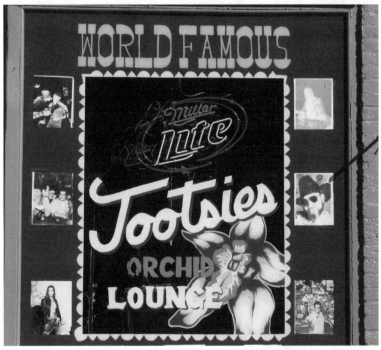

Honky-tonk Tootsies Orchid Lounge,
lower Broadway, Nashville.

A Personal Journey

My first trip to Nashville was back in 1997. I was attending the National Association of Music Merchants (NAMM) trade show. Trade shows, as a rule, are grueling endeavors. A lot of time is spent on your feet, shaking hands and talking. By the third day of the trade show grind I needed a break. I was eager to step out and see what Nashville had to offer. The Nashville convention center is located in the heart of downtown Nashville, so it was a matter of minutes before I was passing by the honky-tonks along lower Broadway. I wasn't hungry, having had a hearty Southern breakfast that morning of grits, biscuits and gravy, and eggs. Nashville was a new world for me and I was more interested in hearing some music than eating. As I left the convention center I took it slow. There was a slight hint of barbecue in the air. It was July in Nashville, and a flickering billboard flashed 102 degrees. With several choices of honky-tonks, I decided to duck into Tootsies Orchid Lounge. The name alone piqued my interest. The façade of Tootsies was painted purple. On the window was the name Tootsies along with colorful painted wild orchids. As I entered, a live band was playing to the left of the bar on what is probably one of the smallest stages in Nashville. The aura of the place took hold immediately. Faux-gold-framed black-and-white photos of country music legends lined the walls. I felt transported, as if in a time warp.

By this I mean outside in the blistering sun it was 1997, but inside Tootsies it was 1960 and cool. The musicians on stage were dressed in plaid country shirts with sleeves neatly rolled up to the elbow. To complete that look, they wore blue jeans, cowboy boots, and hats. They were playing country standards like "Folsom Prison Blues" by Johnny Cash and "Walking the Floor Over You" by Ernest Tubb. Since I'm not from Nashville, this was a new experience, true Americana, and I thought to myself, "I'd love to play a gig at Tootsies one day."

Originally called Mom's, Tootsies Orchid Lounge was purchased by Hattie Louise "Tootsie" Bess in 1960 and quickly became a meeting place for singer-songwriters. Country stars like Willie Nelson and Faron Young hung out at Tootsies. Roger Miller's hit song "Dang Me," primarily about a guy down on his luck, spending all of his money on drinks, was supposedly inspired by him hanging out at Tootsies as well.

After an hour it was time for me to get back to the trade show, but something had changed in me. I was hooked. I spoke with a friend later that day as the trade show came to an end. I said to her, "I could really see myself living here in Nashville one day."

Ten years later I played my first gig at Tootsies. It was July, which could only mean one thing: It was hot and beyond humid. That same flickering electronic billboard sign showed a temperature of 90 degrees at 8:00 P.M. But this time it was me up on that stage— without the plaid shirt and cowboy hat, mind you. I had joined a country cover band and prepared for that gig by listening to hundreds of country music songs. I listened to Nashville's premier country music station, WSM 650 AM, which plays everything from Ferlin Husky to Carrie Underwood. WSM also broadcasts the *Grand Ole Opry* live every Friday and Saturday night.

Listening to WSM 650 AM was an education all its own, and I would highly recommend, as a newcomer to Nashville, listening to that station religiously, especially in the evenings with Eddie Stubbs. Stubbs has a smooth, authoritative voice and knowledge about country music and artists that is mind-boggling. The gig I played that night at Tootsies was not without drama. At the last minute one of our guitar players bowed out. We needed a replacement—a gun for hire who either knew the cover songs we had chosen or was good enough to pick up the songs on the fly. Most musicians who play the honky-tonks in Nashville have a strong working knowledge of at least fifty to seventy country songs in their arsenal. The guitarist we found was no exception. As we say these days, he had mad chops. We didn't know this guy, and it turned out he had some problems with the law. Nothing too serious, but halfway through our set two cops came up on stage, motioned to us to stop playing, and arrested our hired gun on the spot. During the cuffing and removal process, I had a chance to take in the crowd standing in amazement, watching what was taking place on stage. This unexpected pause in our set gave me time to reflect back to the first day I had entered Tootsies ten years earlier. My life had changed. I had started a small music production company, found a job in the music business on Music Row, and was now playing Tootsies. In many ways the gig that night was a dream come true. We finished our set with "Fishin' in the Dark" by the Nitty Gritty Dirt Band. After packing up our gear we made our way to the bar for a post-gig beer. As musicians, we look forward to that moment, an opportunity to speak openly about what songs worked or didn't, engage in familiar banter like, "I thought we were a bit slow in this song," or, "Man, your solo was spot-on."

However, all we could say that night was, "I can't believe the cops arrested our guitar player!" That was a new one for me. We had played a good set, made money for the bar at Tootsies, and now had a Nashville gigging story all our own.

Finding Your Way

When I first set up shop in Nashville, I was amazed by how welcoming Nashvillians were. When I would tell people that I had just moved here their eyes would light up and they'd say, "Welcome to Nashville." For me this went a long way. To this day, whenever I return from a trip, the response is the same. Every once in a while I'll even get a "Welcome home." So, to keep that good vibe going, I'd like to welcome you to Nashville. My own move to Nashville took place on a cold, snowy day. I had packed up my rent-a-truck the night before, and, at 6:00 A.M., with the truck crammed with personal belongings and musical instruments, I was off. Like many before me I was leaving my home, my comfort zone, venturing out toward a new life. As I drove, the sun broke through early-morning clouds. As I made my way further south, thoughts of what my new life would be like preoccupied my mind. Who would I meet? Where would I work? Would I get into a band? I would need to furnish my place, buy a car and tools to assemble furniture. My journey and a whole host of new challenges were just beginning.

The first piece of business was finding a place to live. Each morning over breakfast at a local Waffle House I would scour the classified sections of local newspapers. I finally found a place along the Cumberland River located about fifteen minutes east of downtown Nashville. Once I arrived, the days and nights that followed were spent going through a laundry list of things that needed to be taken care of. Moving to Nashville was the easy part. Getting settled and finding my way would be the real test.

What I realized after conducting several interviews for this book and speaking with songwriters from a wide range of backgrounds is that moving to a new city and trying to establish yourself takes guts, discipline, and sheer determination. In all of my years of travel I have never seen such a sense of community among songwriters and musicians as I do here in Nashville. Several singer-songwriters I spoke with expressed the same feeling that if "one of us gets a break [in this competitive music scene], we feel like we've all succeeded."

As musicians, we all make our own musical journeys. Writing this book for me was no exception. As when writing a song, I started out with an idea, a few lines to build on. On some days, things just didn't seem to fit, but on others, the words would flow, and soon the book began to take its own shape and form. So, to a large extent, this book is my song that I present to you. Nashville can be a strange town at times and you'll hit roadblocks and experience moments of frustration. Helping you follow your dream and hone your craft as a songwriter and musician is the purpose of this book. I hope my experiences of getting settled here in Nashville and finding my way will help you find yours, allowing you to take full advantage of all the things this great music city has to offer. With all of my support, I wish you the best of luck.

CHAPTER 2

Nashville: A Brief History

Busking for tips on lower Broadway, Nashville.

The Beginnings

No matter where people go, they always take their music and instruments with them. This was no different for the first settlers who came to this country and specifically to the southeastern part of the United States. To understand and appreciate the development of any place, I have found that it helps to know a little bit about its history and how that place came into being. Since this book is all about Nashville, Music City, this will be a musical history. Over the years the words *music* and *Nashville* have become synonymous. In some ways, what you will experience as you prepare to move to Nashville is similar to what the original settlers went through. Granted, there have been significant improvements over the years, such as indoor plumbing. However, at the core, you are moving, with your instrument, whatever that might be, and you are looking to connect and start a new life. I've always believed that experience yields content and that content becomes your life's song.

The music that developed in the southeastern region of this country resulted from the blending of songs from the settlers' native homeland with new songs about the challenges that faced them. These early songs served as a foundation and were like homemade recipes passed from generation to generation. These songs would inspire new musicians to put their own unique spin on them. As with any recipe, however, new elements were added, and at the heart of country music lay certain key ingredients. The lyrics are straightforward, and the themes of these songs for the past hundred years have centered on everyday life. Motifs of faith, family, love, betrayal, hope, and loss, are still echoed in some of country music's most popular hits today. A good example of this musical foundation would be an early recording by the Carter Family called "No Depression in Heaven," recorded in 1935. This song spoke directly to the hardships of the Depression era of the 1930s, tapping into the theme of faith and the idea that those who struggled would one day be rewarded a place in heaven.

Over time, these early songs would go through a metamorphosis, being changed and adapted in accordance with their new environment and shifting local influences. The instruments that settlers brought with them were as important to them as the tools they used to harvest the crops. As communities grew, so did the desire to write new songs. This new form

of music being developed and played in the foothills of the
Appalachians and further west in Nashville would eventually
become known as country music.

Nashville was named after General Francis Nash, who
fought in the American Revolution. The city was originally
called Nashborough; the "ville" was then added later in
honor of the French, who came to the aid of the United
States during the war.

These days that early music is referred to as "old-time music."
The instruments that were employed came from around the world;
the dulcimer, the mandolin, and the banjo, from western Africa, all
came together in the creation of a new indigenous American music
art form. This new blending and incorporation of music and musical
instruments would serve not only as a comforting reminder of
where the settlers came from but acted as a map to where they were
going in the new frontier. In order to know how we got where we are
today, we need to look back.

To understand how Nashville became Music City, it is helpful to
look at three major components: the Ryman Auditorium, WSM 650
AM radio, and the *Grand Ole Opry*. The Ryman is held in high regard
by musicians around the world not only for its history but also its
remarkable acoustics. As many audience members have stated over
the years, "There's just not a bad seat in the house." The radio station
WSM 650 AM has more or less served up a country music format for
eighty-five years, and the *Grand Ole Opry*, which was established
in 1927 has aired, without interruption, more than 4,500 shows
and counting. Today, pretty much every musician who comes to
Nashville dreams of having his or her songs played on WSM 650 AM,
of performing live on the Ryman stage, or of being part of a Friday or
Saturday night performance on the *Grand Ole Opry*. Whether you're
a singer-songwriter or in a band, getting a chance to do one of those
three things is the bellwether of success in Nashville.

Music for the Masses

With the introduction of "amplitude modulation," or AM, radio in the early part of the twentieth century, music found a new powerful distribution tool. This new technology changed the way in which people listened to music, and paved the way for country music to reach a wider audience. As a historical footnote, in 1920, KDKA AM Pittsburgh broadcast the Warren Harding/James Cox presidential election results. This was a first. Soon afterward, the station began running a variety of radio programs on a daily basis. In 1924 the first country song to have nationwide success was a song called "The Wreck of the Old 97," recorded by Vernon Dalhart.

> If you listen and watch carefully, in the 1980 film *The Blues Brothers*, Elwood Blues, played by Dan Aykroyd, apologizes to the owner of the country music venue Bob's Country Bunker for not performing the "The Wreck of the Old 97."

The Birth of Country Music

In 1927 a record producer and talent scout for Victor Records named Ralph Peer headed to Bristol, Tennessee, a small city situated at the foothills of the Appalachians. He was out making "field recordings." His job was similar to that of an A&R representative at one of today's record labels, searching for new talent. On that trip he discovered Jimmie Rodgers. Rodgers had been a railroad brakeman, but in 1924 he contracted tuberculosis and decided to pursue his passion for music. Rodgers's musical style encompassed the folk music that he grew up with, mixed with African-American blues and his signature "yodeling" style. Because of this Rodgers is affectionately referred to in country music circles as the "Singing Brakeman" or "America's Blue

Yodeler." Rodgers is credited with being the "Father of Country Music" and was the first performer to be inducted into the Country Music Hall of Fame. The recordings "Blue Yodel No.1 (T for Texas)," "Sleep Baby, Sleep," and "Blue Yodel No. 9," the last of which was recorded in 1930 and features Louis Armstrong on trumpet, are three examples of Rodgers's musical style.

> In 1935, Patsy Montana (born Ruby Blevins) was the first female country music singer to sell a million copies of a single, with "I Want to be a Cowboy's Sweetheart."

On that same trip Peer also discovered a family trio, the Carter Family, who were looking to record. Peer's meeting with the Carter Family and Jimmie Rodgers at this time is considered by many as the "big bang" moment for country music. The Carter Family trio was made up of a husband-and-wife team, A. P. Carter (Alvin Pleasant Delaney Carter) and Sara Carter, and her cousin Maybelle Addington, who played guitar. A. P. Carter's claim to fame was taking traditional folk songs that were abundant in neighboring small Appalachian villages and communities and reworking their lyrical and musical structures. Other factors that were important to the trio's unique sound were Sara Carter's voice and Maybelle's guitar playing. Maybelle's unique guitar stylings can be heard on the trio's first recording, 1927's "Bury Me Under the Weeping Willow." Maybelle would eventually marry A. P. Carter's brother Ezra and give birth to a daughter, June, who would have an incredible music journey all her own, eventually marrying country music legend Johnny Cash in 1968. Call it fate, serendipity, or divine intervention: This meeting in 1927 in Bristol, Tennessee, between Peer, Rodgers, and the Carter Family would be the bedrock on which country music would be built.

In 1941 the Carter family was photographed for *Life* magazine, one of the leading national publications, at the time. A photo of them with an editorial feature would have meant even greater exposure for the trio. However, a week before the issue was to be published, Pearl Harbor was attacked. The article was never printed.

WSM 650 AM—"The Air Castle of the South"

In October 1925, WSM 650 AM radio broadcast for the first time from Nashville, Tennessee. The radio station was the brainchild of Edwin Craig, who was an executive at the National Life and Accident Insurance Company headquartered in downtown Nashville. The call letters WSM stand for "We Shield Millions." The radio station and studio were located on the fifth floor of the National Life, building which no longer stands. The idea behind creating a radio station was simple. It gave the National Life and Accident Company a way to reach new policyholders on a greater scale, and it offered a way for advertisers to reach people living in hard-to-reach rural areas.

With that in mind, let's jump ahead two years to 1927. In that year WSM's radio signal was amped up, so that the station was able to cast an even wider net, reaching millions more people in 38 states and even some parts of Canada. So, with Peer signing new talent such as Jimmie Rodgers and the Carter Family, it was only a matter of time before the blending of a strong radio signal and a lineup of star performers would come to a head.

In the mid-1970s, Pat Sajak was a DJ at WSM 650 AM before joining—say it with me—*Wheel of Fortune!*

Country music legend Minnie Pearl.

The *Grand Ole Opry*—The Longest-Running Radio Program in American History

The *Grand Ole Opry* was an idea most credited to George D. Hay. Hay had come from Chicago, where he was a well-known radio announcer at WLS radio. Its call letters stood for "World's Largest Store," referring to its owner, Sears, Roebuck and Company. Live music variety shows called barn dances were very popular at this time. Instead of offering the same old barn dance format, Hay wanted the *Opry* to showcase country music stars. The show was an instant hit, thanks to Hay, its well-known host, and the successful music acts it featured. Country artists were now coming to Nashville not only to play the *Grand Ole Opry* but to make recordings of their songs as well. What's important to keep in mind is that although there were other stations around the country at that time broadcasting a wide range of music and entertainment programs, the geography of Nashville played a major role in the *Opry*'s success. Think of it this way: Tennessee is surrounded by seven states—Arkansas, Mississippi, Alabama, North Carolina, Virginia, Georgia, and Kentucky. So, performers could gig out in these other states during the week, hitting multiple markets, and still make it back to play the *Opry* and be on the radio in Nashville on Saturday nights.

STRINGBEAN

David Akeman, aka "Stringbean," was a banjo player who became a member of the Grand Ole Opry and was a cast member on the popular TV show *Hee-Haw*. After a live performance on the *Grand Ole Opry* at the Ryman in November 1973, Stringbean and his wife, Estelle, drove back to their home. It had been rumored that Stringbean, being a product of the Depression, stashed large amounts of cash in his house. On that fateful night a pair of gunmen broke into the house and both Stringbean and his wife were slain. The next day the couple was discovered by another *Hee-Haw* fixture and the couple's neighbor, Grandpa Jones.

Ryman Auditorium: "The Mother Church of Country Music."

The Ryman Auditorium— "The Mother Church of Country Music"

The Ryman Auditorium first opened its doors in 1892 under its original name: the Union Gospel Tabernacle. In 1904 the name was changed to the Ryman Auditorium in dedication to Captain Tom Ryman, who owned a fleet of steamboats in Nashville and was instrumental in getting the Union Tabernacle built. Originally used for religious services, the building eventually became home to the *Grand Ole Opry*. The Ryman was home to the *Opry* from 1943 to 1974, during which time music legends such as Little Jimmy Dickens and Elvis Presley played on its stage. By the late 1940s and early 1950s, with established stars such as Ernest Tubb, Hank Williams, Hank Snow, and Lefty Frizzell, country music was on the fast track to becoming the largest-selling genre of music in the nation.

In 1951, Ernest Tubb opened his record store in Nashville, which is still in operation today, across the street from the honky-tonk bars and the Ryman Auditorium on lower Broadway. I spoke with Ernest Tubb's biographer Ronnie Pugh, and he said that the music being produced after World War II and before the introduction of rock 'n' roll represented, in his opinion, the golden age of country music. However, by the late 1950s country music was at a crossroads. The Nashville Sound emerged and was in direct response to the popularity of rock 'n' roll. Recordings by Jim Reeves, Patsy Cline, Eddy Arnold, and Marty Robbins marked the beginning of a sound that was more polished and commercial, with the use of backing vocals and string arrangements. A quintessential example of the Nashville Sound would be Patsy Cline's (born Virginia Patterson Hensley) "Walking After Midnight."

Will the Circle Be Unbroken?

Coming full circle, the song "Will the Circle be Unbroken," originally recorded by the Carter Family, still remains country music's perennial anthem. The song serves as a constant reminder of those who have come before and the continuation of tradition and of creating music. The institutions that have made Nashville "Music City" still stand today. WSM 650 AM radio, the *Grand Ole Opry*, and the Ryman Auditorium remain the cornerstones and symbols of how powerful country music has become.

DISCOVERING NASHVILLE'S MUSIC HISTORY

To get a further sense of how Nashville became home to country music, I highly recommend visiting the following establishments that are fascinating in their own right and will help give you a deeper sense of how country music developed over the decades.

Country Music Hall of Fame
Ryman Auditorium (backstage and museum tour available)
RCA Studio B (tour available)

Making the Scene—Nashville Listening List

Early Country Music Recordings:

Vernon Dalhart, "The Wreck of the Old 97"

Fiddlin' John Carson, "The Little Old Log Cabin in the Lane"

Jimmie Rodgers, "Blue Yodel No. 9"

The Carter Family, "Will the Circle Be Unbroken"

Patsy Montana, "I Want to Be a Cowboy's Sweetheart"

Hank Williams, "Lovesick Blues"

Ernest Tubb, "Walking the Floor Over You"

Hank Snow, "I'm Moving On"

Kitty Wells, "It Wasn't God Who Made Honky Tonk Angels"

Lefty Frizzell, "If You've Got the Money, I've Got the Time"

One of Patsy Cline's most famous songs, "Crazy," was written by Willie Nelson.

Country Music History Timeline, 1892–1984

1892 Union Tabernacle/Ryman Auditorium opens its doors for religious services.

1925 WSM 650 AM broadcasts for the first time from Nashville, Tennessee.

1927 Ralph Peer, a talent scout for Victor Records, discovers Jimmie Rodgers and the Carter Family in Bristol, Tennessee.

1927 George Hay introduces the barn dance variety format to WSM 650 AM radio and creates the Grand Ole Opry.

1933 "The Father of Country Music," Jimmie Rodgers, dies at the age of 35.

1943 The Grand Ole Opry moves to the Ryman Auditorium, where it will stay until 1974.

1947 Bluegrass is introduced with Bill Monroe's release of "Blue Moon of Kentucky."

1949 Hank Williams records "Lovesick Blues."

1953 Hank Williams dies at the age of 29.

1954 Elvis Presley and rock 'n' roll are introduced to the world and country music is forced to reinvent itself.

1954 Johnny Cash records for the first time at Sun Studio in Memphis.

1960 The Nashville Sound is in full force. With the introduction of strings and backing vocals, the Nashville Sound was a cleaned-up version of country music featuring artists such as Patsy Cline, Eddy Arnold, Ray Price, and George Jones.

1961 The Country Music Hall of Fame is established and inducts Jimmie Rodgers and Hank Williams. Willie Nelson writes "Crazy" which becomes one of Patsy Clines biggest hits.

1963 Patsy Cline dies in a plane crash at the age of 33.

1964 Charley Pride becomes the first African-American country music star.

1970 Bill Monroe and the Carter Family are inducted into the Country Music Hall of Fame.

1974 The Grand Ole Opry moves from the Ryman Auditorium to its new home, the Grand Ole Opry House, located at Opryland, just outside of downtown Nashville.

1976 Willie Nelson introduces the outlaw movement with the release of the album *Wanted: The Outlaws*, which includes vocals by Johnny Cash, Waylon Jennings, Hank Williams Jr., and Kris Kristofferson. This album was the first country music album to sell one million copies.

1980 Countrypolitan is introduced, and a new set of stars such as Reba McEntire and George Strait emerges.

1982 The Bluebird Cafe opens in Nashville, becoming one of the most important venues in Nashville for songwriters and launching many careers, such as that of Garth Brooks.

1984 Ralph Peer is inducted into the Country Music Hall of Fame.

Throughout the book I've interviewed music industry professionals who work with songwriters every day in Nashville. It's my hope that these interviews will help you better understand the best approach and how to be prepared for launching your songwriting and music career.

Interview:
Sheree Spoltore, Vice President, Membership Services, NSAI (Nashville Songwriters Association International)

Liam Sullivan: What should a musician, singer, or songwriter do before they come to Nashville?

Sheree Spoltore: Preparation is the most important thing. Having talent is only 10 percent of the equation. Being knowledgeable about how the music business works should be at the top of your list. Music is a business built on talent but at every point of development you have to learn your craft. [As with] every other kind of vocation, you have to be trained: Whether you're a plumber or schoolteacher, you have to become certified to do that. It's the same thing for songwriters. One of the biggest misconceptions that songwriters have is they think to themselves, "I can sing; I've got a song and good looks," and then they wait for someone to discover them. That's the wrong approach.

LS: How does becoming an NSAI member help a songwriter become prepared for learning the ropes in the music business so they become, as you said, "certified"?

SS: Through our website, we teach you how to network before you even get to Nashville. A lot of people quit their jobs and move their families here without any knowledge of how the music scene in Nashville works. That's not balanced, that not a business plan— that's more like a Hail Mary play. There are very few things you would ever do in life that would make you drop everything and move somewhere without having some knowledge of what you're getting yourself into.

LS: Can I join NSAI from my hometown and how much would that cost me?

SS: Yes, you can join from wherever you are in the country. A yearly membership is $150 and you can pay that in three $50 installments. Once you do that, you can submit your songs and one of our professional songwriters will give you feedback and help you develop your songwriting skills. However, we have over 160 NSAI workshops across the nation, and you can find that list for your city on our website. It's a great support system and a great way to prepare before you ever move to Nashville.

LS: Okay, so I've done my research and I'm now living here in Nashville. Now what?

SS: You can come to NSAI with your songs and questions and we will sit down with you and get a sense of who you are and your specific needs. Each songwriter/musician is different—it's not cookie-cutter. So we figure out the best approach and we mentor you by listening to your songs, and we give you suggestions on how to "trim the fat," as a music publisher would say, and help you with lyric structure [and] verse-chorus contrast. So we act as a conduit between you and the publishing companies here on Music Row. Years ago songwriters would walk up and down Music Row and knock on doors and pitch their music. It doesn't work that way anymore. [Here at] NSAI we can help you get your songs heard because we deal with all the major song and music publishing companies, and if we like what we hear, we will pitch your song or songs.

LS: Can you explain how the mentoring program works here at NSAI?

SS: With your membership, you have two free one-on-one mentoring sessions with one of our staff, and that person will help you put together your own plan as a songwriter. We also have singer-songwriter workshops here at NSAI every Thursday night at 6:30 that you can attend. It's a great opportunity to play your songs and network with other musicians here in Nashville.

LS: What other services does NSAI offer?

SS: We have online educational tutorials that you can access when you become an NSAI member. These tutorials have music industry decision makers telling you how to take a music publishing meeting, how to license your music out to film and TV. We have over two hundred webcasts that singer-songwriters can watch at their leisure and [use to] get educated on how to get started in the music business. Whether you're here in Nashville or not.

LS: So I've gone through the mentoring program and have attended the Thursday night workshops and I've watched the tutorials on the NSAI website. How do I get to the next level?

SS: Your music is going to tell us a lot about who you are and how far along you are with your craft. All of our staff here are songwriters, so we understand what you're going through. We tell you the truth. Maybe your vocals are weak, so you need to work on that, or maybe you're a very good lyricist but your song structure needs work. So before you go and make a demo and spend that money, we can help you get to the level of performance. The first thing we do is make sure that your songs are the best they can be. Once that happens, we teach you how to co-write with other people. One great tip is to sit down and make a list of twenty songs that you wish you had written. A lot of songwriters lack definition and direction, so that's a great exercise to help you focus and to get a better sense of the kind of songs that you want to write. We also offer a Pitch to Publisher program.

LS: How does the Pitch to Publisher program work?

SS: Once a quarter, throughout the year, we host a Pitch to Publisher luncheon, and we play NSAI members songs for Nashville music publishers. The songs we pitch are by members who have compiled a good-size catalog of original songs, and this is because we have to show the music publishers that you can write good songs consistently.

LS: Okay, so you play a songwriter's song at a Pitch to Publisher luncheon and there is a song that a music publisher likes. Then what happens? Can I get a publishing deal from that?

SS: NSAI gets you ready to get to that level to make that connection. So let's say they like a song. We make the call for you and make that introduction, and now you're ready to start a relationship with that music publishing company. They might want to set you up with one of their hit songwriters and see how you fit in with what they're doing. Think of it as dating: They want to feel you out and see if you've got the goods and if there is the right chemistry.

LS: Let's say that goes really well and there is good chemistry. How do I make money?

SS: At that point, NSAI doesn't really get involved with the final negotiations. That is now between you and your music publisher. But usually what happens is the following: Publishing deals these days work off a draw, 18-18-18, which means eighteen songs delivered over eighteen months for $18,000. However, these days it's more like $12,000, based on songs that a publisher agrees to take on in their catalogue. The money, however, is a loan, and once one of the songs sells, the sales go up against the $12,000 that the music publisher loaned you. It's an advance and not free money.

LS: Can you explain what a song plugger does? And does NSAI pitch songwriters' songs to song pluggers?

SS: Yes, we have contact with several song pluggers here in Nashville, and we can make recommendations. The song plugger takes the song to established artists, producers, managers, and A&R people. So if you are accepted to join a music publishing company and you're co-writing with someone at that music publishing company, your chances are better to get a song into the hands of a song plugger, who will most likely go to the big artists like Tim McGraw, Reba, or Carrie Underwood, as well as other music industry folks.

LS: What other advice would you give to a singer-songwriter who comes to Nashville to pursue their dream?

SS: First, get prepared to hear a lot of no's, and I'll say this again: Managers, labels, the PROs [peformance rights organizations], and producers all want to work with people who are knowledgeable about how the music business works. They want to work with people who have a vision of what it is they want to do. Don't wait for someone to define you; define your sound, your image, and your vision of what it is you want to do. In the music business, you have to remember the three R's: Relationships, Revenue, and Results. NSAI can give you that knowledge and help you get to the next level. And even when you have one hit single, you have to repeat that, so it's a lot of work. The more understanding of the business and your craft [you have], the better off you'll be.

LS: What if I'm not a good songwriter but I have a great voice? How can NSAI help me?

SS: NSAI can help you get demo work and introduce you to songwriters who write great songs but need that great voice. Getting into the studio and working behind the microphone, you can work with engineers who will supply you with tips on how to market your voice and what the best fit for your voice is. It could be pop, Americana, or country. Engineers eventually become producers, so you want to establish relationships with them. It's important to remember that NSAI services every genre of music, whether it's Latin, hip-hop, rock—it's not just country.

LS: What other tips can you suggest to songwriters who have moved to Nashville?

SS: Go to all the music organizations here in Nashville and do the research find out who they are, what they do. Try and make a contact and ask questions at places like the musicians' union [American Federation of Musicians], NARAS [National Academy of Recording Arts and Sciences], all the PROs. If you need a guitarist or a drummer, we have access to that information, so you can build out a band. We give you tips on how to create merchandising and how to make the most out of playing a gig and also how to get a gig that is right for you and your sound. Like I said earlier, people want to work with people who have a thorough knowledge of not only the music business but also who they are as an artist and performer.

Settling In

CHAPTER 3

**❝Gotta get back to Nashville
'Cause that's where the good times are❞**
—The Everly Brothers, "Nashville Blues"

Back in the early 1960s, a struggling musician trying to make it in Nashville was living in a one-room loft but was determined to get his guitar chops up to snuff and to play out. The story of young musicians coming to Nashville to pursue their music career is nothing new, and this kind of story plays out on a daily basis here in Nashville. That musician back in the early '60s who was trying to make the big time was none other than guitar great and rock 'n' roll icon Jimi Hendrix.

Before you make your move I highly recommend that you make a checklist. Thorough preparation before you move is key. A good place to start is the Nashville Area Chamber of Commerce website. There you will find information regarding jobs and apartments, as well as helpful tips for those thinking of moving to Nashville. If you're planning to start a small business, e.g., Bob's Music Production, the chamber provides information that can help you get that up and running as well. The goal is to gather as much information as you can before you land, so that you can establish yourself in Nashville as easily and as quickly as possible.

Resources for Making Your Move

Nashville Music City Convention & Visitors Bureau

The Nashville Music City Convention & Visitors Bureau and the chamber of commerce are a stone's throw away from one another. As I mentioned earlier, this is also a great place to get a free map, and to delve deeper into all that Nashville has to offer. The staff is well informed and very friendly.

150 Fourth Ave. N., Ste. G-250

Nashville, TN 37219

(800) 657-6910

www.musiccityusa.com

Nashville Chamber of Commerce

211 Commerce St., Ste. 100

Nashville, TN 37201

(615) 743-3000

www.nashvillechamber.com

In 1939, NBC TV started broadcasting a half-hour show of the Grand Ole Opry, reaching millions of people across the country and increasing country music's popularity.

Getting Here and Around

Airport

Flying into various airports across the country can be a hassle, with long lines, flight delays, and boarding gates that are so far apart you practically need to take a flight to get from Terminal A to Terminal C. Not the case in Nashville. A good word to describe flying into Nashville's BNA airport is *seamless*. It also doesn't hurt that there always seems to be a slight hint of barbecue in the air when you come off the plane and into the terminal.

Nashville International Airport

Airport Code: BNA

One Terminal Drive

Nashville, TN 37214

(615) 275-1675

www.flynashville.com

Shuttles from the Airport

Nashville Express Shuttle

This shuttle services all the hotels in downtown
Nashville from the airport.
Call for reservations and information, or visit their website.
(615) 335-6479
www.nashvilleexpressshuttle.com

While researching and writing this book, I received numerous suggestions from people who have made the move to Nashville. Many said that coming here first for a short trip is the way to go instead of picking up and just moving. By visiting you can get a feel of the place without committing, and flights to Nashville are relatively inexpensive. So take your time, make the small investment, get a sense of the city and where you think you would like to live. Then, with that information, go back home and make a detailed plan of attack. However, if you're throwing caution to the wind and moving to Nashville without having a place to move into, I've listed some clean and inexpensive hotels from which to choose. Some hotels offer great deals on rooms equipped with a kitchenette, Internet, and other amenities that won't put a dent in your wallet.

Hotels

Brentwood Suites
622 Church St. E.
Brentwood, TN 37027
(615) 277-4000
www.brentwoodsuite.com
$69.33 per night
Free Internet, free parking, free breakfast

Extended Stay America
2525 Elmhill Pike
Nashville, TN
(615) 883-7667
www.extendedstayamerica.com
$39.99 per night
Includes kitchenette, free parking. Internet and breakfast not included.

Ramada Inn Nashville
2425 Atrium Way
Nashville, TN 37214
(615) 883-5201

www.ramada.com

$55 per night

Kitchenette, free Internet, free breakfast, free parking

> **66 It was my sixteenth birthday; my mom and dad gave me my Goya classical guitar that day. I sat down, wrote this song, and I just knew that that was the only thing I could ever really do. Write songs and sing them to people. 99**
> —Stevie Nicks

Car Rental

I always thought renting a car at the airport was cheaper. Not so in Nashville. Avoid that at all costs or you'll end up paying through the nose. There are plenty of locations throughout the city that you can get to from the airport by taxi, and it will only cost you about $30. I've supplied both the 800 number and local numbers for most of the major car rental places. The reason for the local number is that I find it helps to speak with someone in Nashville who has a solid knowledge of the inventory, especially if you're looking for a specific car or van. Not all rent-a-car companies have a downtown location, so I've only listed the ones that do. If you forget to make a reservation before you leave, you can always go up to the rent-a-car companies' desks at the airport and ask to make a reservation at one of their downtown and less expensive locations.

Budget

1816 Church St.

Nashville, TN 37203

(800) 527-0700

(615) 366-0806

www.budget.com

Enterprise

2214 Eighth Ave. S.

Nashville, TN 37204

(800) 261-7331

(615) 279-5604

www.enterprise.com

Hertz

3100 Charlotte Ave.

Nashville, TN 37209

(800) 654-3131

(615) 327-5453

www.hertz.com

Thrifty

1201 Briley Parkway

Nashville, TN 37217

(800) 847-4389

(615) 361-6050

www.thrifty.com

Two red twins.

Word on the Street
with Nashville Songwriter Julie Forester

Hometown: Longview, TX

Liam Sullivan: What was your experience like moving to Nashville?

Julie Forester: I dove right in as soon as I got here. I joined ASCAP and NSAI [National Songwriters Association International] and started writing, singing, and working a regular job. I remember feeling like I had found my real home in Nashville.

LS: What advice would you give other musicians who are thinking of moving to Nashville?

JF: Make sure this is really what you want to do, because it is a very long and hard road. You have to love it to stick it out. There are very few overnight successes, but if this is all you want to do, then come on and get to work.

LS: Describe your favorite Nashville moment as a musician.

JF: It would have to be the night I first played the Bluebird Cafe. I had worked there on and off as a waitress for a few years, so when I finally got the chance to play a writers' round at the Bluebird Cafe, I felt a sense of accomplishment, even if only for a night.

Public Transportation

Taxi Services

Each of these cab companies has minivans in its fleet. So if you find yourself without wheels and need to get to your gig on time with all your gear, these guys can help.

Allied Cab

(615) 883-2323

Checker Cab

(615) 256-7000

Nashville Cab

(615) 242-7070

Yellow Cab

(615) 256-0101

Buses

It has to be said that there is something romantic about the notion of arriving by bus to a town like Nashville. Guitar strapped on your back and ready for whatever comes your way. It also must be said that it's probably been a while since the words *romantic* and *Greyhound bus* have been used in the same sentence. Regardless, if you don't have that far to go, taking the bus can be an affordable way to travel and a good way to see some of the country while you're at it. Not to kill the moment, but once you get off the bus in Nashville, you will most likely have to take a cab to wherever it is you're going.

Greyhound Bus Station Nashville

1030 Charlotte Ave.
Nashville, TN 37203
(615) 255-3556
www.greyhound.com

Speaking of buses, not everyone has a car, and many folks rely on Nashville's MTA to get them to and from work. Their website offers detailed routes and maps and carpooling options. Local service will run you $1.70, while express buses are $2.25. You can purchase your ticket (Metro fare card) in advance on their website. An all-day pass costs $5.25; a seven-day pass is $24; and a monthly pass is $84. Drivers do not make change on the bus.

Metropolitan Transit Authority (MTA)

130 Nestor St.

Nashville, TN 37210

(615) 862-5950

www.nashvillemta.org

Finding a Place to Live

Before you start gigging out, certain practical things need to fall into place. Finding a place to live is most likely top priority on your list. The great thing about Nashville is that there is an abundance of affordable housing. Many people think that when they move to a city they have to live in the center of the action. That's not the case in Nashville. There are plenty of neighborhoods in and around Nashville that are very affordable and easily accessible to downtown and Music Row. A prerequisite for many musicians moving to Nashville is striking a balance between living quarters and a practice space. Like a lot of cities, Nashville is made up of many smaller neighborhoods. Each has its own feel and unique offerings. I've asked several musicians living here in Nashville what they were looking for in a neighborhood when they moved here. Their answers were virtually the same: "I want a place that is fairly centrally located, with cool bars, restaurants, and live music venues, and I want to feel safe." The one thing that I will continually stress throughout the book is that you are here to establish yourself and to create what I would call a "musician's life," so I would argue that you want to surround yourself with other musicians who share your passion. Since I moved here, there have been plenty of Friday and Saturday nights sitting around with friends listening to, playing, and sharing music. To a large extent, you want to make your own scene. Where you end up living can play a big part in your new Nashville life. Another perk about living in Nashville is that music is all around and plays a big role in everyday life. Throughout downtown there are outdoor speakers strategically placed playing country hits all day and night. On lower Broadway live music starts at 11:00 A.M. in the dimly lit but inviting interiors of the honky-tonks. At night, in all of the neighborhoods that I've written about here in this chapter, there are open mic nights and music industry showcases, and artists of all musical genres can be found performing in local venues. Therefore, the goal here is to highlight Nashville's most popular neighborhoods and break down the benefits of living in each one.

Rentals

Renting a place in Nashville is affordable, and a good-size house or apartment can cost between $600 and $1,400 per month. I found my place looking through the classified section of the local newspaper the *Tennessean*. If you hunt for a place online, there are all sorts of services that say they're Nashville-based, but you will soon learn they offer more regional listings. You want Nashville-specific. Everyone's story about how they found a place when moving to Nashville is different, but if you're looking to get settled, you need as many resources as possible at your disposal to get settled into your new digs.

Resources

I know it's hard to believe, but in this digital age, the best place to find a place to live in Nashville is the *Tennessean*. The advantages to this are multiple. Their classified section is spot-on, with lots of great rental listings by owners, thus allowing you to avoid paying a finder's fee or a finder's commission. The other advantage is that by flipping through the paper you get a sense of local politics, cultural events, and the latest on Nashville's sports teams. Wait a minute! We're musicians, not jocks! Right you are, but if you're going to live in Nashville, it's hard *not* to become a supporter of the Tennessee Titans (the local football team), the Nashville Predators (the local hockey team), or the Triple-A baseball team, the Nashville Sounds. If you don't want to get black smudge on your fingers, the *Tennessean* also has a website.

The *Tennessean*
1100 Broadway
Nashville, TN 37203
(800) 342-8237
www.tennessean.com

Apartment Finder
(800) 222-3651
www.apartmentfinder.com

Apartment Selector
(800) 394-2736
(615) 833-3151
www.aptselector.com

If all else fails, alternative options could include a cardboard box, a tent, or, yes, even Craigslist.

Craigslist
www.craigslist.com

HELPFUL TIP

Get a map of Nashville and hang it on your wall, where it will serve as a great visual aid. Finding a place takes time. You will most likely spend a fair amount of that time running around checking out different neighborhoods. Here's the best approach: Pick a neighborhood on your map. Highlight that area and then cross-reference it with the classified listings in local newspapers or online rental sites. Maps of Nashville are easy to come by at the airport, hotels, gas stations, and bookstores, or you can print one out online.

Largest honky-tonk ascot!
Lower Broadway, Nashville.

Best Neighborhoods for Musicians in Nashville

Downtown

Think of downtown Nashville as the hub in a wheel. This is the center from which all things branch out. On any given weekend, lower Broadway is alive with flashing neon lights, live music, and a bustling bar and restaurant scene. The honky-tonks are the main attraction and a good place to see live bands playing mostly well-known country covers. Living downtown can be a bit more expensive than some of the other neighborhoods in and around Nashville. For the cost of renting a one-bedroom apartment downtown, you can rent an entire house in other parts of the city. Second Avenue and lower Broadway make an L shape. Second Avenue is comprised mainly of old warehouses that were once the main storage units for dry goods coming into Nashville along the Cumberland River. Today, these warehouses have been transformed into lofts and condominiums on the top floors, with bars and restaurants taking up most of the storefront spaces below.

East Nashville

To get to East Nashville you have to cross the Cumberland River. There are a few ways to do this, including swimming, but the best way is to take the Woodland Street bridge, which will bring you right into what is known as "5 Points," the heart of East Nashville.

The Family Wash music venue, East Nashville.

East Nashville has gone through a renaissance of sorts in the past few years. Once considered the "bad" side of town, this neighborhood has flourished into a bustling new bohemia. Musicians and artists of all stripes have made this area their new home mainly because it is so affordable. Because of that, a vibrant mix of singles, young families, and musicians has changed the face of East Nashville, almost demanding the invasion of hip new bars and restaurants. East Nashville is made up of a series of small neighborhoods with names like Lockeland Springs, Edgefield, and Inglewood. There is a renewed sense of energy and excitement about this area that will make any newcomer feel right at home, and it is only minutes from downtown.

Word on the Street
with Nashville Songwriter Ryan Michaels

Hometown: San Francisco, CA

Liam Sullivan: What brought you to Nashville?

Ryan Michaels: I came here to study at Belmont University. I majored in music business and took courses in publishing and commercial performance. I also took voice lessons and guitar lessons, which gave me a great foundation for my songwriting.

LS: What advice would you give to other musicians who are thinking of moving to Nashville?

RM: First and foremost be focused and have a real sense of what you're trying to do with your music. The other thing is, if you get a meeting with a music industry person, give them your pitch, but always ask for advice. By asking for their advice you're getting a chance to hear what they think of your music: Sometimes that can be even more valuable and make all the difference. In this town, just listening can sometimes be the best educator.

LS: What other advice would you offer up?

RM: After you take a meeting with someone in the music industry, always follow up with a handwritten thank-you note and drop it in the mail. Eventually, if the relationship is good enough, it will turn into something more, and more opportunities will come. The other thing is that you have to be all in. You can't dabble as a songwriter in this town. You're competing with people who are 100 percent committed, so you can't have one foot in, one foot out.

LS: How have you developed your music career here in Nashville?

RM: I'm an independent artist, so I can't compete with a major record label. I can't afford to hire a radio promoter to pitch a couple of my sides [songs] to promote my music on major radio. What I can do, however, is go after Internet and college radio and secondary formats, because that's realistic. I've also pursued licensing out my music to film and TV, because oftentimes film and TV companies don't want to license music out from major record labels because it can be incredibly expensive.

LS: How have you built a following for your band?

RM: I've created a database of e-mails from all the shows I've done with my band across the country. I keep in constant contact and engage people through my website who have come to our gigs. The most important thing that I do is I try and thank everyone who came to my shows. People have invested their time to come and see me, so I have to show the utmost appreciation.

LS: Seems a lot of musicians I meet have a "Nashville" story when it comes to their music careers. What's yours?

RM: I was interning at a music publishing company and came across a CD that everyone had taken a pass on. It was just sitting at the bottom of this box. I gave it a listen and liked it. I saw the contact info on the CD, picked up the phone, and called the guy whose CD it was. We started co-writing together, and eventually he took me to a producer, which in turn got me a co-publishing deal through EMI. Fast-forward: I just put out my first CD, and the guy whose CD everyone took a pass on back then wrote two of the singles with me. So it's all about loyalty and working with people you believe in.

LS: Sounds like Nashville karma.

RM: [*Laughs*] Yes, karma is very much alive in this town.

LS: Describe your perfect Nashville day.

RM: I go to Radnor Lake a few times a week to walk: It helps with working out songs in my head. I love getting together with other songwriters during the day and then going out to the Station Inn to see live music. But the biggest thrill I get, however, is [from] having a community of friends that I get to play and record with.

Hillsboro Village/West End/Music Row

The name says it all. Hillsboro is indeed a village, which to me means everything you need is within walking distance. The village boasts everything from a French bakery to used-book shops and is home to the Pancake Pantry, where Nashvillians are willing to wait on line outside in any kind of weather just to get their pancake on.

Located near Vanderbilt University, Hillsboro Village is teeming on most days with college students, musicians, and Music Row professionals, who make good use of some the best restaurants in town, like the Sunset Grill, during lunchtime.

Hillsboro is a great place to walk, grab a coffee, or get a late-afternoon beer with a friend at another neighborhood landmark, Jackson's, located right on Twenty-First Avenue.

The Historic Belcourt Theatre, Hillsboro Village, Nashville.

BELCOURT THEATRE

Built in the 1920s, the Belcourt was originally a silent movie theater; it was home to the Grand Ole Opry from 1934 to 1936. Today the Belcourt serves as a live music venue and revival cinema offering independent, foreign, and classic films in every genre. Besides serving up popcorn, which is ubiquitous at any movie theater, the Belcourt also has a good selection of local beers from the Yazoo Brewing Company and mixed drinks to keep you perky.
2102 Belcourt Ave.
Nashville, TN 37212
(615) 383-9140
www.belcourt.org

Germantown

Germantown is located just north of the Capitol building, so it's still close enough to downtown that the area has an inner-city vibe. It is located near the farmers' market and the Bicentennial Capitol Mall, which is a great place to go for a stroll on the weekends. Tucked in between Jefferson and Hume Streets, Germantown is one of

Nashville's oldest neighborhoods, which makes for an interesting diversity of architecture that appeals to a wide range of working professionals and musicians alike.

Berry Hill

Nashville's smallest neighborhood, Berry Hill is only one square mile, to be precise. It is considered by many to be a mini Music Row. Recording studios are plentiful, and there are cool shops, which make this city within a city a very attractive and musician-friendly part of town. There are several hip clothing shops that offer everything from current to vintage apparel. Berry Hill is also home to one of Nashville's best record shops, Phonoluxe, which specializes in vinyl and all the latest music releases.

A Little Bit of Gospel

66 There's more women stars in Nashville all the time. They're proving they can do the job the same as a man. 99 —Loretta Lynn

Sylvan Park

Located in the western part of town, Sylvan Park consists of comfortable and affordable bungalows, which are perfect for a small family or a single musician. Most of these bungalows have basements, which is a major plus for setting up a rehearsal or practice space. The one thing that distinguishes Sylvan Park from other neighborhoods is that all the streets are named after states (Nevada, Michigan etc.). So it's like living in two states at once. Sylvan Park has a residential feel while still being close enough to both Charlotte Pike and the trendy and hip West End.

Green Hills

Green Hills is a bit pricey, but its location is prime in that it's near Hillsboro Village, West End, and Music Row, so you're really in the thick of where the music happens. There is also the Mall at Green Hills, which is one of the best shopping malls in Nashville. Because the homes in this area tend to be larger, there are often rooms for rent, which gives you the opportunity to live at an upscale address without paying upscale prices. The only drawback is that by renting a separate living space within a larger house, you'll have to keep your noise level to a minimum. But with the Bluebird Cafe located nearby, it might put the fire under your bum to get out and play live.

CHARLIE POOLE

Banjo player Charlie Poole is often overlooked and even sometimes forgotten, but in many respects, his contribution to country music is legendary. Many music historians believe that his unique banjo playing was a direct influence on the development of bluegrass and Bill Monroe, "The Father of Bluegrass" himself. Poole's recording of "Don't Let Your Deal Go Down" with the North Carolina Ramblers, recorded in New York City in 1925 for Columbia Records, is a good example of Poole's banjo and vocal stylings.

Buying a House

If buying a starter home in Nashville is more what you're looking to do, here are the most recent listings and price ranges by neighborhood.

East Nashville and Inglewood:	$95,000 to $130,000
Berry Hill:	$180,000 to $220,000
Hillsboro Village/West End:	$275,000 to $325,000
Music Row :	$280,000 to $320,000
Sylvan Park:	$150,000 to $200,000
Germantown:	$250,000 to $300,000

Testing, one, two, three. Mic the
bike stand, Music Row, Nashville.

Utilities

Nashville Electric Service (NES)

1214 Church St.

Nashville, TN 37246

(615) 736-6900

www.nespower.com

Nashville Metro Water

1700 Third Ave. N.

Nashville, TN 37208

(615) 862-4600

www.nashville.gov/water

For all other utility inquiries, visit the city government's comprehensive website.

Metropolitan Government of Nashville

(615) 862-5000

www.nashville.gov

Recycling

Large items often come in big boxes. Once the excitement of removing the large item from the big box is over, there is that moment when you say to yourself, "I gotta get rid of all these big boxes!" Here's how.

Metro Nashville Public Works

(615) 880-1000

www.nashville.gov/pw/recycle

Internet and Cable

For cable, landline, and Internet hookups, Comcast offers affordable bundled packages allowing you to mix and match whatever services you might need.

Comcast Cable

660 Mainstream Dr.

Nashville, TN 37228

(615) 244-5900

www.comcast.com

Local Banks

First Tennessee

965 Woodland St.

Nashville, TN 37206

(615) 227-7411

www.firsttennessee.com

Regions

315 Deaderick St.

Nashville, TN 37201

(615) 748-2091

www.regions.com

SunTrust

201 Fourth Ave. S.

Nashville, TN 37219

(615) 748-4576

www.suntrust.com

Furniture

Once you've found your place, you'll need to furnish it. Some people bring all of their stuff with them in a rent-a-truck while others pack just the essentials and furnish their places when they get here. If you're on a budget, which most musicians seem to be, then there is no better place for all your needs than Big Lots! They carry everything from sofas to plates to canned sardines, if that's your thing. You can furnish an entire bedroom and get some living room furniture, all for about $500. Everything is discounted. All the time. If that's not your style, I've listed plenty of other places for all your couch potato and furnishing needs.

Big Lots
3734 Annex Ave.
Nashville, TN 37209
(615) 352-1297
www.biglots.com

Big Lots
1137 Gallatin Pike S.
Madison, TN 37115
(615) 860-1102

Ashley Furniture
2160 Gallatin Pike N.
Madison, TN 37115
(615) 855-3339
www.ashleyfurniturehomestore.com

Remix Furniture Used Furniture
1004 Eighth Ave. S.
Nashville, TN 37203
(615) 736-7515
www.remixfurniturestore.com

Rooms to Go

2253 Gallatin Pike N.

Madison, TN 37115

(615) 851-1201

www.roomstogo.com

Rooms to Go

8103 Moores Lane

Brentwood, TN 37027

(615) 373-4144

SWEDISH MEATBALLS, ANYONE?

The closest IKEA to Nashville is the one in Atlanta. The drive will take you about three hours and you want to leave early because Atlanta traffic is notorious for being a nightmare in the afternoons, evenings and even on the weekends. Let's face it it's never a good time so make sure to stock up on all of your favorite Kungsbacka, Narvik, and Ingmar furnishing needs while you're there.

IKEA Atlanta
441 16th St. N.W.
Atlanta, GA 30363
(404) 745-4532
www.ikea.com

Sprintz

325 White Bridge Pike

Nashville, TN 37209

(615) 352-5912

www.sprintz.com

Southern Thrift

5010 Charlotte Ave.

Nashville, TN 37209

(615) 292-1807

www.southernthriftstore.com

Southern Thrift

412 Metroplex Drive

Antioch, TN 37211

(615) 833-1319

Southern Thrift

2701 Gallatin Pike

Nashville, TN 37216

(615) 228-1368

Performance rights organization
SESAC, Music Row, Nashville.

Interview:
Tim Fink, Vice President, Writer Relations, SESAC

Liam Sullivan: How is SESAC different from the other performing rights organizations such as ASCAP and BMI?

Tim Fink: SESAC develops a relationship with writers before they are affiliated. They aren't just a number. This allows SESAC to work more closely with the affiliate on their individual needs rather than just trying to appeal to the masses. SESAC is also a technological leader among the nation's performing rights organizations, and I think it's important to mention that we utilize top digital technologies to enhance the tracking of performances. Another way we're different is that SESAC, by design, is the smallest of the three U.S. performing rights organizations. Because of our size and our selectivity, SESAC offers more efficient and personalized services [that] are unique to the industry. Our size allows SESAC to be deeply committed to the continuing professional development of our affiliates. Additionally, there are no fees for SESAC services or any cost to become affiliated.

LS: Please explain the process of how one becomes affiliated with SESAC.

TF: SESAC has an open-door policy when it comes to becoming a SESAC affiliate. You will not, however, find an application online or [be able] to simply request an application, as SESAC actually wants to find out more about you by listening to your music, or have a meeting with you to begin to develop a relationship to determine if affiliation would be mutually beneficial. SESAC is a selective organization in this manner and takes pride in having a repertory based on quality, rather than quantity. You can begin this process by contacting one of the SESAC writer/publisher relations departments in New York, Nashville, Atlanta, Miami, or Los Angeles, whichever is most convenient to your region.

LS: What happens if I get turned down by SESAC? Can I try to become affiliated later on? How many strikes do I get before SESAC takes a pass on me and my songs?

TF: There is no number of "strikes" you get before SESAC takes a pass. SESAC is looking for potential affiliates that need what our company offers, which is the representation of the public performance of your songs. Oftentimes writers will look to affiliate with a performing rights organization well before they need the service and then become bound by the terms of the contract with that PRO. If your songs are being performed [and] you are not in control of [that], then that is a good indicator that you might need an organization to represent them on your behalf.

LS: What advice would you give to a singer-songwriter who is thinking of moving to Nashville to pursue a music career?

TF: This is a decision that has to be made on a case-by-case basis. While this may be the right decision for some, it may not be for others. You must truly define your purpose for making this decision. You should spend time coming to Nashville just as a visitor: Some singer-songwriters do this for years before making the commitment to move here on a permanent basis. In my opinion, the best approach is to develop relationships here in Nashville and experience the competition that already exists before making the move.

LS: In your opinion, what would be some of the do's and don'ts for songwriters when they first get to Nashville?

TF: Do your homework. Be persistent. Don't become an annoyance. This is a very fine line.

LS: Does SESAC put on showcases around town highlighting their songwriters? If so, could you explain what those are like?

TF: SESAC hosts showcases around town highlighting their songwriters. We're here to support all of our affiliates in any way possible.

LS: Are there workshops at SESAC so a songwriter can improve their chops and or find a co-writer to work with?

TF: There are workshops for SESAC songwriters where networking occurs that could potentially lead to developing a relationship with another songwriter.

LS: How does SESAC find new members? Do SESAC representatives go out to open mic/writers' nights to find new talent?

TF: As is true in many areas of the industry, the majority of the writers that get signed [do so through] their relentless networking. Through that networking process, writers often get introduced to SESAC from other industry professionals that could be publishers, other songwriters or managers. Generally, when industry professionals are at a showcase, or at an open mic event, it is because they have a purpose for attending: They know who they are going to see, and not because they are just going to "scout" unknown talent.

LS: What are some successful traits that you've seen in singer-songwriters that gave them a better shot at succeeding in music in Nashville?

TF: You can't look at this as a job. It isn't. It is a lifestyle. There are so many variables to be successful, and you get to only be in control of one of them, which is the quality of your music. Your music has to be at the highest caliber. All the rest is about the other variables lining up at the right time and place. There is no formula. As far as traits, I would recommend the following: networking, persistence, networking, humbleness, networking, a relentless work ethic, networking, being able to accept rejection, and one more thing which I might have forgotten to mention, networking. And even then, it might not work out.

Mattress/Futon Stores

Fluffo Mattress

901 Woodland St.

Nashville, TN 37206

(615) 227-2751

www.fluffo.com

Futons, Futons, Futons

610 Thompson Lane

Nashville, TN 37204

(615) 242-8666

www.futonsx3.com

Mattress Express

2412 Antioch Pike

Antioch, TN 37013

(615) 669-8886

www.mattressexpressnashville.com

Mattress Warehouse

2107 Murfreesboro Road

Nashville, TN 37217

(615) 361-7852

www.mattresswarehousenashville.com

Mattress Warehouse

4648 Old Hickory Blvd.

Old Hickory, TN 37138

(615) 679-9077

Mega-Marts

Kmart

4095 Nolensville Rd.

Nashville, TN 37211

(615) 833-2231

www.kmart.com

Kmart

1508 Gallatin Pike S.

Madison, TN 37115

(615) 865-0040

Target

6814 Charlotte Pike

Nashville, TN 37209

(615) 238-0112

www.target.com

Walmart

4040 Nolensville Pike

Nashville, TN 37211

(615) 831-0133

www.walmart.com

Discount Stores

There are certain household items that don't need a flashy logo.
"Why pay more!!" as the slogan goes, when all you need is the generic product, sometimes in bulk, and as cheap as you can get it.

Dollar General

3776 Nolensville Pike

Nashville, TN 37211

(615) 831-2175

www.dollargeneral.com

Dollar General

2101 Eighth Ave. S.

Nashville, TN 37204

(615) 297-5557

Elvis lives! Outside RCA Studio B,
Music Row, Nashville.

Flea Market

Nashville Flea Market

Mixing and matching new furniture and classic Americana items can sometimes make for a good conversation starter in your new place. At the Nashville Flea Market there is something there for every eclectic and not-so-eclectic taste. I once found an old circus diagram with a plastic bear dancing with a ladder. Americana indeed!

The flea market is held the last Saturday of every month at the Tennessee State Fairgrounds, which are conveniently located near downtown Nashville and are accessible to all the major highways.

625 Smith Ave.

Nashville, TN 37203

(615) 862-5016

www.nashvilleexpocenter.org

Admission: Free

Parking: $5

Malls

Not only are they great places to get a cinnamon bun, these malls have all the big department stores that we've all come to know: Dillards, Macy's, Nordstrom, and the like. They are also filled with shops and boutiques that cater to every buying desire.

CoolSprings Galleria

1800 Galleria Blvd.

Franklin, TN 37027

(615) 771-2128

www.coolspringsgalleria.com

The Mall at Green Hills

2126 Abbott Martin Road

Nashville, TN 37215

(615) 298-5478

www.themallatgreenhills.com

Rivergate Mall

1000 Rivergate Parkway

Goodlettsville, TN 37072

(615) 859-3456

www.rivergate-mall.com

Electronics/ Appliances

As we all know, most rentals come equipped with refrigerators and washer-dryer units, but sometimes a 72" plasma TV in the middle of your living room just makes the place feel more like a home. All of these places have great deals, especially around holidays and presidential birthdays, so try and plan accordingly.

Best Buy

2311 Gallatin Pike N.

Madison, TN 37115

(615) 859-0115

www.bestbuy.com

Electronic Express

2714 West End Ave.

Nashville, TN 37203

(615) 329-1700

www.electronicexpress.com

Electronic Express

21 White Bridge Rd.

Nashville, TN 37205

(615) 352-4510

hhgregg

719 Thompson Lane

Nashville, TN 37211

(615) 259-3344

www.hhgregg.com

hhgregg

2190 Gallatin Pike

Madison, TN 37115

(615) 851-3841

Everyone has a story, and often those stories find their way into song. In my travels going out to gigs, music showcases, industry meet-and-greets, and writers' nights, I've met a wide range of musicians who have come to Nashville to pursue their dream of making music, writing songs, and hoping for that big break. I have found that hearing other people's stories and adventures about music or travel is beneficial. It gives me insight, and often I can learn from those who have come before me, giving me a better understanding of the hurdles and accomplishments that they have faced.

Some of the people I have interviewed here in this book offer up their own unique stories, which I hope will give you a better perspective on what it will take to move to Nashville and create your own musical community. Some of the stories are of struggle, but at the end of the day it was these people's music, their songs, that made them dig deep and follow their passion. It is my hope that by reading about their journeys you will come away with a new perspective and, most important, with the realization that you are not alone and that you can make Nashville whatever you want it to be.

Interview:
Jeff King, Guitarist for Reba McEntire

Hometown: Townsend, TN

Liam Sullivan: When did you first start playing guitar?

Jeff King: I found a guitar in my uncle's closet when I was about ten, and I picked it up and I just loved the sound. Not sure what tuning it was in but I was fascinated. Soon after that, my mom got me a few guitar lessons with a local singer-songwriter guy in town, and the first song I learned to play was the old folk song "Wildwood Flower" by the Carter Family. Playing that guitar became the thing I loved to do, so I started listening to records and would slow the record player down and I'd try and play what I heard on my uncle's guitar. As a young kid I just remember loving the way music made me feel. Finally, my parents bought me an electric guitar and a small Fender Vibro Champ amp, which I still have. I had cousins who played bluegrass on the weekends, so music was all around me at that age. After that, as a teenager I got into Southern rock and started creating little leads on the guitar, which I was pretty proud of, and as that developed I started working on my tone, trying to create different sounds so that I could play a variety of songs.

LS: When did you decide to come to Nashville, and what was that experience like?

JK: After college I came to Nashville to pursue a career in music. I worked in a warehouse to make ends meet, but I would go out pretty much every night and watch what other guitarists were up to. That was a great learning experience, because I realized that I needed to get to work if I wanted to be as good as some of the guitarists that I was seeing. I would also approach guitarists that I thought were good after a gig and introduce myself. I began to learn the names of producers that were producing albums here in Nashville, so I did my homework, networked, and in a sense gained a solid knowledge of how the music scene worked.

LS: What was your first break as a musician here in Nashville?

JK: I had joined a cover band and we did some original material, but for the most part we played country and pop music, and we toured around in other states, which was a good experience, because we would play night after night in front of a different audience. Because of that, my playing got a lot better. Because of the networking I was doing and the amount of people I was meeting, I got a call from a buddy of mine one day who said that Patty Loveless was putting a band together and was auditioning guitarists for an upcoming tour. So I went and auditioned.

LS: What was that process like?

JK: I was terrified. I brought my own gear because I have found over the years that it's important to have a comfort level when you're trying to be creative. When you audition you want to make sure that how you play and what you play is a true representation of your sound. So I had a set time to swing by and audition for Patty. I played a couple of songs and luckily I got the gig. But it's important to remember that that audition didn't happen overnight. I had done my homework and networked with a wide range of people: All of that was vital to getting the audition with Patty and that then led to going out on a national tour with her.

LS: How did you get the gig playing with Reba?

JK: I did some session work on songs that landed up on a few Reba albums. One day Reba's guitarist [Jerry McPherson] left to pursue other interests. I knew all the guys in the band really well from the sessions I did, so they asked me if I wanted the gig and to tour with Reba. "Of course," I said so I learned the songs, did rehearsals, and hit the road.

LS: What's a day in the life like for a touring musician?

JK: Depending on where we are on tour, sometimes the other musicians and I will rent a car and take in what the place has to offer, maybe grab some lunch. But most days we've got to get to sound check by four o'clock. After that we'll goof around and have some dinner. Before the show I'll change clothes, check my gear and make sure everything is ready before I hit the stage. After the show we'll all have a beer and hang out, but pretty soon it's back to the tour bus to crawl into our sleeping bunks and we take off in the middle of the night toward the dawn and the next gig.

LS: What has been your favorite moment as a Nashville musician?

JK: There was a day years ago when I got the chance to play for Don Williams, Michael W. Smith, and Ricky Skaggs all in the same day. I think that day was in a way a crowning achievement, to be able to play different genres of music with three great musicians. There was a feeling of wonderment that I was able to have that chance.

LS: Describe your perfect day in Nashville.

JK: I love waking up around 6:30.

LS: Wait a minute, 6:30? You're a musician right?

JK: [*Laughs*] Yeah, well, it takes all kinds, I guess. But I love that time of morning. I make some coffee, play my guitar for a while just to loosen up. Then by about ten or so I head off into the studio to play with my buddies and do some recording; then we'll grab some lunch, which is something we love to do. The fact that I have that chance to be creative with friends and to do that on a daily basis is just incredible.

All roads lead to the Loveless Cafe!

Buying a Car

There are plenty of used-car dealerships in the metro Nashville area, and to be honest, having bought a couple of used cars in Nashville myself, the process can be unsettling, to say the least. Even with a CarFax report, buying a used car can still be a risk. Once it's off the used-car dealership's lot, there's no going back. There's a saying that a lot of used-car dealerships in Nashville use that goes "We Tote the Note," which basically means that they will stretch the dollar to get you in the car you want and get you the best deal.

Here are some tips on how to best protect yourself:

- Get the dealer to print out the CarFax report.
- Get the VIN (vehicle identification number) and go online to Kelley Blue Book to see what the car is really worth at. www.kkb.com.
- Also try Edmunds, at www.edmunds.com, which is another helpful third-party resource and offers information about tools and services as well.

Be prepared to spend at least an additional $500 once you buy the car. Why? Because there's a very good chance that you will need a new battery and tires, and possibly pads and shoes for your brakes. So add that into the total cost of what you're willing to spend.

CarMax

2353 Gallatin Pike N.

Nashville, TN 37115

(615) 855-2202

www.carmax.com

Music City Motors

Online-only classified listing of used cars for sale in the Nashville area

www.musiccitymotors.com

DMV Plates and Emissions Tests

The first thing you need to do before you can get your license plates is to have your car undergo an emissions test, which is sometimes referred to as MARTA. It's quick and inexpensive $10. After your vehicle has passed inspection, you can go and get your plates, which will cost you $80. The sticker you receive is good for one year, at which point another emissions test is required.

Nashville Emissions Testing Centers

North Nashville

34934 Dickerson Road

Nashville, TN 37207

www.nashvillevip.org

West Nashville

501 Craighead St.

Nashville, TN 37204

East Nashville

715 Gallatin Pike N.

Nashville, TN 37115

Nashville Department of Motor Vehicles

Downtown

312 Rosa Parks Blvd.

William R. Snodgrass Building, 3rd Fl,

Nashville, TN 37243

(615) 532-9780

North Nashville

624 Hart Lane

Nashville, TN 37216

(615) 532-9780

West Nashville

6604 Centennial Blvd

Nashville, TN 37209

(615) 741-4560

"Extra, Extra!"

Finding a Job

The reality is that while you're making your way, meeting new people, recording and gigging out, there is the practical side to life, which is paying the bills. It's the least glamorous bit, but here's a listing of places that can get you placed working flexible hours and not leave you drained at the end of the workday. If these don't work out for you, a lot of musicians I know work in restaurants and bars, which by their very nature are great places to make money and meet people.

Accountemps

315 Deaderick St., Ste. 1500

Nashville, TN 37238

(615) 385-2600

www.accountemps.com

AmTemps Staffing

2636 Elm Hill Pike, Ste. 300

Nashville, TN 37214

(615) 885-6500

www.amtemps.com

Express Employment

2210 Rosa L. Parks Blvd.

Nashville, TN 37228

(615) 313-3690

www.expresspros.com

Office Team

315 Deaderick St., Ste. 1500

Nashville, TN 37238

(615) 292-4600

www.officeteam.com

Personal Appearance

66 You'd be surprised how much it costs to look this cheap! 99
—Dolly Parton

Hair Salons

Wash, cut, highlight, repeat. Looking good for a gig is as important as rehearsing. Looking as if you just rolled out of bed while still looking cool is a hard thing to accomplish. So leave it to the pros.

Element

2002 Richard Jones Rd.

Nashville, TN 37215

(615) 727-8484

www.elementsalonnashville.com

Escape Day Spa & Salon

6000 Hwy 100, Ste. 102

Nashville, TN 37205

(615) 352-3545

www.escapespaces.com

Green Pea Salon

2900 12th Ave. S.

Nashville, TN 37204

(615) 297-6878

www.greenpeasalon.com

Lucy Pop Salon

1921 Broadway

Nashville, TN 37203

(615) 327-3474

www.lucypopsalon.com

Salon FX

1915 Broadway

Nashville, TN 37203

(615) 321-0901

www.salonfxspa.com

There also may be certain gigs that don't require you to look like a million. So if you just want to get some highlights, a quick trim, or a Mohawk to shake things up, all at an affordable price, Super Cuts is your best bet. They have several locations throughout Nashville and beyond. Here are some of their centrally located salons.

Super Cuts

7058 Charlotte Pike

Nashville, TN 37209

(615) 353-0047

www.supercuts.com

Super Cuts

2059 Scarritt Place

Nashville, TN 37203

(615) 341-0140

Super Cuts

519 Donelson Pike

Nashville, TN 37214

(615) 391-4288

Spas

Nashville is probably one of the least stressful cities in the country, but no matter: Sometimes you just have to pamper yourself. These guys can help you melt away that stress.

Massage Envy

8024 Highway 100

Nashville, TN 37221

(615) 662-3689

www.massageenvy.com

Natural Oasis Day Spa

2214 Elliston Place, Ste. 100

Nashville, TN 37203

(615) 515-3767

www.naturaloasis.com

Interview:
Julie Roberts, Nashville Recording Artist

Hometown: Lancaster, SC

Julie's single "Break Down Here" was a Top 20 single on *Billboard*'s Hot Country Songs chart.

Liam Sullivan: What was your experience like moving to Nashville?

Julie Roberts: Well, I always knew I wanted to move to Nashville because eventually, all songwriters look to Nashville—it's a songwriter's town. It's where country music legends recorded and made their careers happen, and everyone wants to be a part of that. I wanted to move to Nashville after high school but my mama wanted me to get a college degree. So I looked for a college in Nashville. I found Belmont University and was determined to get in and major in music business. I didn't know anyone in Nashville, so my move here was exciting and scary at the same time. It was also difficult because I didn't have a lot of extra money for food. Mama would send me boxes of food every single week so I could eat.

LS: How did you network and meet other musicians? Did you play open mic nights?

JR: A large majority of students at Belmont are musicians, writers, singers, producers, so it was very easy to meet people in school. Outside of school was a little more difficult. My college roommate helped me take my press kits, tapes, and CDs to all the venues in town to try and get gigs. I finally got booked at a few coffee shops, a pizza restaurant, and a Laundromat called Harvey Washbangers. [*Laughs*]

LS: Those sound like some pretty unconventional and tough gigs to pull off. Was it nerve-racking?

JR: Well, I've always loved being on stage, so playing these places was a lot of fun for me. But I guess I was always a little nervous because at every show I had hopes that someone from a record label would be there, love my music, and sign me on the spot!

LS: Even at a Laundromat?

JR: In this town you always have to expect the unexpected. You never know who you're going to meet or where an opportunity will come from next. Even if that means singing over the noise of a washing machine spin cycle. [*Laughs*]

LS: What advice would you give to singer-songwriters who are already out of college and are thinking of moving to Nashville?

JR: Come on! It's not going to find you. You have to get here and find your dreams. Go to shows, meet songwriters, singers, producers, and be brave. Ask them if they'd like to write with you. Ask them to listen to your music. Keep showing up and be prepared to give them a CD of your work if they ask to hear it. Go out on a limb and call people for meetings. The worst thing they can tell you is no.

LS: What are the do's and don'ts of getting yourself involved in the music scene in Nashville?

JR: Do know who you are and what you want. Don't take no for an answer. Don't stop taking your demos around town. Do try to sing, play, and write every single day. Don't ever give up.

LS: What was your first big break in Nashville regarding your music career?

JR: After I graduated from college I was hired on full-time as the receptionist at Mercury Records. I answered phones during the day and sang at venues and wrote songs at night. I had a CD and was looking to shop it around and get a record deal. During that time I was promoted to be the assistant to the chairman of UMG (Universal Music Group), Luke Lewis. I also started working with one of Nashville's best-known guitarists, Brent Rowan, who has worked with George Strait, Sting, and Alan Jackson, etc. We recorded some songs we loved and began to shop them around to A&R [artist and repertoire] folks around town. Initially they told Brent they "didn't get it," they didn't get my sound. But Brent never gave up and neither did I. One day Brent said to me, "Would you feel comfortable if I played our recordings for your boss, Luke?" I told him, "Okay, but please don't tell my boss it's me singing unless he likes it because I could get fired." It was a bold move but I also needed the paycheck. So I set up the meeting between my boss, Luke Lewis, and Brent. I told my boss that Brent was working with some new artists and he wanted to play some songs for Luke. Luke agreed. When Brent arrived for the meeting with Luke, Luke shut his office door and I could hear my music playing through the walls. Halfway through the first song, Luke turned the song off. I thought, "Damn, he doesn't get me either." But that wasn't it at all; Luke said, "Who is this girl? I want to meet her." Brent said, "It's the girl sitting right outside your office answering the phones." Shortly after, I signed a development deal with Mercury Records and released my debut album.

LS: What are some of the things you feel that you did differently that made all the difference in separating yourself from the thousands of other singer-songwriters in Nashville who were trying to do the same thing as you when you first started out in your career?

JR: I didn't set out to be different from anyone else. I just set out to do music that I loved. Being yourself is very important and probably why I was told no more than a few times. It is too stressful to try and sound like someone else. Being honest in your music and who you are is way more rewarding.

LS: Can you describe the feeling you had when you first heard your hit single "Break Down Here" on the radio?

JR: I was on the treadmill at the gym the very first time I heard "me" on the radio. I about shit my britches on that treadmill. I kept running faster and faster and I smiled the whole time. After it was over I got off and called Mama! It was what we had dreamed about my whole life.

Tattoos

Need some color in your life? Found an Asian symbol that miraculously sums up your entire philosophy? Or maybe that quote from Yeats really would look better on your forearm. Regardless, whatever your tattoo needs, the key is that when you decide to get one the tattoo shop is clean and has a long list of satisfied customers. Here's a list of places that will hopefully ink you in the right direction.

Billy Joe's Tattoo

301 Broadway

Nashville, TN 37201

(615) 256-4278

No website so swing by or give 'em a call.

Black 13

209 10th Ave. S., Ste. 218

Nashville, TN 37206

(615) 750-3741

www.black13tattoo.com

Ink Gallery Tattoo

2204 Elliston Place

Nashville, TN 37203

(615) 321-8777

www.inkgallerytattoo.com

Music City Tattoo

1022 16th Ave. S.

Nashville, TN 37212

(615) 742-8822

www.musiccitytattoo.com

Queen of Hearts

2225 Nolensville Road

Nashville, TN 37211

(615) 256-5051

www.queenofheartstattoos.com

Sophia Quebe, singing at
the Station Inn, Nashville.

Clothes

Levy's

3900 Hillsboro Road, Ste. 36

Nashville, TN 37215

(615) 383-2800

www.levysclothes.com

Clothes for men and women since 1855!

Posh

1801 21st Ave. S.

Nashville, TN 37212

(615) 383-9840

www.poshonline.com

Clothes and shoes for men and women

Two Old Hippies

401 12th Ave. S.

Nashville, TN 37203

(615) 254-7999

www.twooldhippies.com

Guitars, clothes for men and women

Men's Clothes

Billy Reid

4015 Hillsboro Pike, Ste. 104

Nashville, TN 37215

(615) 292-2111

www.billyreid.com

Flip

1100 Eighth Ave. S.

Nashville, TN 37203

(615) 256-3547

www.hip2flip.com

The Label

2222 12th Ave. S.

Nashville, TN 37204

(615) 915-0722

www.thelabelnashville.com

66 Music is the universal language of mankind. 99
—Henry Wadsworth Longfellow

Women's Clothes

Apricot Lane Boutique
315 12th Ave. S.

Nashville, TN 37203

(615) 942-7153

www.apricotlanenashville.com

Clothing Xchange
Hillsboro Village

1817 21st Ave. S.

Nashville, TN 37212

(615) 463-0209

www.nashvilleclothingxchange.com

Flavour
1522 Demonbreun

Nashville, TN 37203

(615) 254-2064

www.flavourclothing.com

Goodbuy Girls
1108 Woodland St.

Nashville, TN 37206

(615) 281-9447

www.goodbuygirlsnashville.com

Hip Zipper Vintage Clothing
1008 Forrest Ave.

Nashville, TN 37206

(615) 228-1942

www.hipzipper.com

House of Stella

1709 Galleria Blvd., Ste. 1007

Franklin, TN 37067

(615) 628-8079

www.houseofstella.com

Ivey Clothes

1200 Villa Place, Ste. 108

Nashville, TN 37212

(615) 679-9088

www.shopivey.tumblr.com

Local Honey

2009 Belmont Blvd.

Nashville, TN 37212

(615) 915-1354

www.localhoneynashville.blogspot.com

Moda

2511 12th Ave. S.

Nashville, TN 37204

(615) 298-2271

www.modanashville.com

Pangaea

1721 21st Ave. S.

Nashville, TN 37212

(615) 269-9665

www.pangaeanashville.com

Pieces Vintage Clothing

211 Louise Ave.

Nashville, TN 37203

(615) 329-3537

No website, so swing on by.

That's Cool

2309 Franklin Pike

Nashville, TN 37204

(615)712-6466

www.thatscool.us

Ryan Michaels, rocking "live" on 8th Ave. South, Nashville.

Jeans

Boutique Bella

2817 West End Ave.

Nashville, TN 37203

(615) 467-1471

www.boutiquebella.com

Imogene + Willie

2601 12th Ave. S.

Nashville, TN 37204

(615) 292-5005

www.imogeneandwillie.com

Shoes for Women

Off Broadway Shoes

118 16th Ave. S.

Nashville, TN 37203

(615) 254-6242

www.offbroadwayshoes.com

The Perfect Pair

2209 Bandywood Drive, Ste. I

Nashville, TN 37215

(615) 385-7247

www.theperfectpairnashville.com

Red Door Shoe Outlet

4004 Hillsboro Pike, Ste. 145

Nashville, TN 37215

(615) 292-2945

www.golcshoes.com

Necessary Nashville

RSS

This is hands-down the best place to get a pair of boots. They've got a huge selection at reasonable prices.

405 Opry Mills Dr.

Nashville, TN 37214

(615) 514-0009

www.rccwesternstores.com

Interview:
Kirsti Manna, Songwriter and Owner of Songwriter Girl

Hometown: Poland, OH

Kirsti has performed live on the road playing keyboards and doing background vocals. She's done gigs on cruise ships, lived in and toured Japan with an all-girl band, and has written hit songs, the most popular being Blake Shelton's hit "Austin."

Liam Sullivan: How did you come to write Blake Shelton's hit song "Austin?"

Kirsti Manna: I was co-writing with a guy named Ashe Underwood, and he had left an outgoing message on his answering machine that said, "If this is Austin, I still love you," because the girl he was in love with had moved back to Austin, Texas. So he was trying to say to her, "If you're calling me from Austin, I want you to know I love you." So I spoke with him at one point and said, "What's with this message on your answering machine? We should write a song!" A lot of people were telling Ashe to write the song but he said to me, if you want to write it you can have it. So I did. Whenever I see him today he still says, "I knew I should have written and stayed with that song!" [*Laughs*]

LS: You never know where a song is going to come from.

KM: That's for sure—you never know. Ideas are all around us.

LS: Even on outgoing voice mail messages.

KM: You bet.

LS: Tell me how Songwriter Girl came about.

KM: Well, in my travels I began meeting tons of people from all walks of life who wanted to know how to become a songwriter, and I had spoken at many events around the country talking about stage performance, troubleshooting when it comes to songwriting and singing a song, and gaining confidence. I had done all that, so I wanted to create events for women. Women are the biggest part of the country music market: They buy the most music and everything else that goes along with it.

LS: What goes on at Songwriter Girl Camp?

KM: We have co-writing sessions and we have informative panels for women songwriters. I wanted to create a sisterhood for women, so we have tips on wardrobe and how to prepare for a photo shoot—all the things that are necessary for creating your image. It's all about the song, but there are all sorts of elements that women need to know about [when] preparing themselves for a career as a songwriter. We also take three songs and break them down in terms of the lyric structure, and we figure out what makes the songs work. We also have mentors who sit down with the songwriter at the camp and talk about their craft and how to improve certain elements when it comes to writing a song.

LS: What advice would you give a songwriter who is thinking of moving to Nashville?

KM: First you have to have a plan. You have to confront your career fear.

LS: What do you mean by that, career fear?

KM: Career fear is confronting the one thing that is preventing you from moving forward. You have to figure out what that is and get it out of the way. You have to be objective about the music you write; you have to build confidence in yourself so you can get out there and be creative and pursue your dream. The other thing is, when you get to Nashville, keep track of the people you meet and always do follow-up: A quick e-mail or handwritten note goes a long way. Think of it as being in business for yourself. Never share a song that isn't ready. You have to always be aware that you are marketing yourself.

Six-string coat of arms,
Gruhn Guitars, Nashville.

Health

Gyms

Like any city, Nashville has plenty of gyms and places to work out. However, the best and most affordable option for Nashvillians is the Centennial Sportsplex located on West End Avenue. This facility offers a full gym, an Olympic-size pool, and a smaller pool for kids. Each locker room is complete with steam and sauna rooms, lockers to store your stuff (lock not included), and showers. There is also an ice skating rink as well as group exercise classes featuring belly dancing, boot camp, yoga at all levels, and step classes. There are outdoor tennis courts and across the street from the Sportsplex is Centennial Park, which has a mile loop for runners and a huge lawn on which you can have a picnic, throw a Frisbee, or sit with your guitar and play.

In the middle of Centennial Park is a full-scale replica of the Parthenon that was built in 1897 to celebrate Tennessee's Centennial Exhibition. The reason for this is that Nashville's other nickname, besides Music City, is "the Athens of the South," because of the many higher educational institutions it boasted back in the 1850s.

Cost of Sportsplex Membership for Residents of Davidson County:

One year: $484

Six months: $247.50

Three months: $137.50

Monthly: $66

One-day pass: $7

Centennial Sportsplex

222 25th Ave. N.

Nashville, TN 37203

(615) 862-8480

www.nashville.gov/sportsplex

Impact Fitness

2300 Charlotte Ave.

Nashville, TN 37203

(615) 321-2300

www.impact-fit.com

YMCA

1000 Church St.

Nashville, TN 37203

(615) 254-0631

www.ymcamidtn.org

Yoga

Hot Yoga
2214 Elliston Place
Nashville, TN 37203
(615) 321-8828
www.hotyoganashville.com

Kali Yuga Yoga
1011Fatherland St.
Nashville, TN 37206
(615) 260-5361
www.kaliyugayoga.com

Steadfast and True Yoga Edgehill
1200-A Villa Place
Nashville, TN 37212
(615) 320-9642
www.steadfastandtrueyoga.com

Willow Pilates
2203 Bandywood Drive
Nashville, TN 37215
(615) 297-7117
www.willow-studio.com

Medical/Health Insurance

Here's a thought: Health insurance offers peace of mind. Here's another thought: Not having health insurance causes doubt, panic, and upset. As musicians, we've got enough to think about, so one easy way to keep your inner hypochondriac at bay is the following.

ASCAP MusicPro Health Care

ASCAP has created MusicPro Insurance Agency for musicians. The easiest way to sign up for this plan is to become an ASCAP member. Not an ASCAP member? No problem. The MusicPro insurance plan offers low-cost insurance for all musicians and anyone involved in the music business. There are several options to choose from that could fit your medical and health care needs. Some of the benefits and coverage include health insurance, life insurance, instrument and gear insurance, tour liability insurance, and discount prescription drug cards.

For more information go to:

www.ascap.com/benefits

www.musicproinsurance.com

Open mic night. The Listening Room, Nashville.

24-HOUR DRUGSTORE

Walgreens
518 Donelson Pike
Nashville, TN 37214
(615) 883-5108
www.walgreens.com

Family and Personal Help Services

Planned Parenthood of Nashville

412 Dr. D.B. Todd Jr. Blvd.

Nashville, TN 37203

(615) 321-7216

www.plannedparenthood.org

Day Care

American Child Care

5508 Corbett Lane

Nashville, TN 37209

(615) 352-6084

Creative Care Center

5820 Hillsboro Pike

Nashville, TN 37215

(615) 665-0153

www.creativecarecenter.com

Holly Street Daycare

1401 Holly St.

Nashville, TN 37206

(615) 227-8252

www.hollystreet.org

Mini Rock Stars Day Care

3123 Kings Lane

Nashville, TN 37218

(615) 299-0466

No website, so swing on by.

Help Line

Tennessee Suicide Prevention Network

295 Plus Park Boulevard, Ste. 201

Nashville, TN 37217

(615) 297-1077

www.tspn.org

THIRD MAN RECORDS

Jack White of the White Stripes opened this all-inclusive recording studio and record shop filled with all sorts of goodies. National acts and artists are invited to record and put out a 7" vinyl recording, which is then put up for sale in the Third Man store. Swing by and who knows? Maybe Jack will even sit on your lap.
623 7th Ave. S.
Nashville, TN 37203
(615) 891-4393
www.thirdmanrecords.com

Food Shopping

The food scene in Nashville has been making major strides in the last few years. It wasn't until recently that Whole Foods set up shop here. Depending on where you land up living in Nashville, a weekly drive over to the farmers' market, where you can stock up on fresh produce at great prices, is worth the trip. The farmers' market also has an eclectic variety of eateries, which is great, because we all know what happens when we go food shopping on an empty stomach. Some of the restaurants include El Mexicano Burrito, Chicago Gyro & Salad Bar, the Original Nooleys, Orient Express, Jamaica Way, Shreeji International Market, and Swett's Restaurant.

Famers' Market

900 Rosa Parks Blvd.

Nashville, TN 37208

(615) 880-2001

www.nashvillefarmersmarket.org

Hours: Mon.–Sun., 8:00 A.M.–5:00 P.M.

Louisiana Seafood Co. at the Famers' Market Bicentennial Mall

900 Rosa Parks Blvd.

Nashville, TN 37208

(615) 499-6865

www.louisianaseafoodco.com

> Sweet chow-chow is pickled veggies and goes with pretty much everything. If you're feeling especially peckish you can even eat it out of the jar. It's a relish, a condiment, a specialty of the South, and a lot of fun to say. So stock up!

Specialty/Organic Produce

East Nashville Farmers' Market

210 10th St. S.

Nashville, TN 37206

www.eastnashvillemarket.com

Hours: Wed., 3:30 P.M.–6:30 P.M.

The Green Wagon

1100 Forrest Ave.

Nashville, TN 37206

(615) 942-7874

www.greenwagonnashville.com

Green, local, tons of stuff.

Harris Teeter Grocery Store

2201 21st Ave. S.

Nashville, TN 37212

(615) 269-7818

www.harristeeter.com

Produce Place

4000 Murphy Rd.

Nashville, TN 37209

(615) 383-2664

www.produceplace.com

Fresh produce and all things organic.

Trader Joe's

3909 Hillsboro Pike

Nashville, TN 37215

(615) 297-6560

www.traderjoes.com

The Turnip Truck

970 Woodland St.

Nashville, TN 37206

(615) 650-3600

www.theturniptruck.com

Whole Foods

4021 Hillsboro Pike

Nashville, TN 37215

(615) 440-5100

www.wholefoodsmarket.com

Crossroads, lower Broadway, Nashville.

Grocery Stores

In all likelihood you will make good use of your local Kroger grocery store. Seems like everywhere you turn there's a Kroger, which is a good thing, because they often have sales on everyday food staples such as pasta, tomato sauce, canned goods, and sweet chow-chow!

Make sure to get a Kroger Plus card, which gets you further discounts on the food you buy. The Kroger Plus card is also honored at various gas stations throughout the city and can save you money

at the pump. So, as the old saying goes, "Eat and get gas"
For store locations, weekly specials, and coupons go to
www.kroger.com.

> In 2011, *Rolling Stone* lauded Nashville as having the
> "Best Music Scene" in the country.

Spirits

Frugal MacDoogal

Eyeing that six-pack and thinking, "That's just not going to be
enough for the kind of blues I got"? Well, not to worry, Robert
Johnson, because this place has everything for the thirsty musician.
Even kegs! There are monthly wine tastings, high-alcohol-content
beers from across the pond, and spirits.
701 Division St.
Nashville, TN 37203
(615) 242-3863
www.frugalmacdoogal.com

Bud's Liquor and Wine Shop

2139 Abbot Martin Road
Nashville, TN 37215
(615) 292-7871
There's no website, so swing by and say "howdy" to Bud.

Midtown Wine and Spirits

1610 Church St.
Nashville, TN 37203
(615) 327-3874
www.midtownwineandspirits.com

Sinkers Wine and Spirits

3304 Gallatin Pike

Nashville, TN 37216

(615) 262-2300

www.sinkerswineandspirits.com

Woodland Wine Merchant

1001 Woodland St.

Nashville, TN 37206

(615) 228-3311

www.woodlandwinemerchant.com

Necessary Nashville

Brown's Diner

There are certain things that can only be found in Nashville, and Brown's Diner has to be near the top of that list. This is a no-frills kind of burger joint, but locals will swear that Brown's has got the best burger in town. So moo it on over to Brown's.

2102 Blair St.

Nashville, TN 37212

(615) 269-5590

No website, so swing on by.

Pets

If there is one thing that Nashville is not in short supply of, it's dogs. A great way to meet new people, network, and allow your dog to make new friends as well is the dog park at Shelby Bottoms Greenway, located in East Nashville. Along with the dog park there is also a four-mile paved loop with rustic trails that go into the woods for mountain biking or an afternoon jog or stroll. And it's all just minutes from downtown.

The entrance to Shelby Bottoms is located at:

2021 Fatherland St

Nashville, TN 37206

(615) 862-8474

www.nashville.gov/parks/nature

ADOPT A PET

If you find that after making the rounds you still haven't made any friends, there is one final option: a pet. They're always happy to see you, and they don't talk back. But if they do, make a recording won't you?

Metro Animal Care and Control
5125 Harding Pl.
Nashville, TN 37211
(615) 862-7928
www.health.nashville.gov (click on "Animal Care and Control")

Pet Care Boutiques

24/7/365 Vet Care

Animal Emergency

2971 Sidco Dr.

Nashville, TN 37204

(615) 386-0107

www.nashvillevetspecialists.com

A Bark Above

1313 McGavock Pike

Nashville, TN 37216

(615) 258-1600

www.abarkabove.net

Come Sit Stay

107 Harding Pl.

Nashville, TN 37205

(615) 352-8600

www.comesitstaynashville.com

Dogtopia

1315 Eighth Ave. S.

Nashville, TN 37203

(615) 736-5700

www.dogdaycare.com

Value Vet

4602 Gallatin Pike

Nashville, TN 37206

(615) 226-3000

www.valuevet.net

Wags and Whiskers

1008 Forrest Ave.

Nashville, TN 37206

(615) 228-9249

www.wagsandwhiskersnashville.com

Nashville Parks

Centennial Park

2598 West End Ave.

Nashville, TN 37203

(615) 862-8400

www.nashville.gov/parks

Percy Warner Park

2500 Old Hickory Blvd.

Nashville, TN 37221

(615) 862-8415

www.nashville.gov/parks

Rocketown

Concert hall, coffee shop, skateboard park you'll never want to leave.

601 Fourth Ave. S.

Nashville, TN 37210

(615) 770-3002

www.rocketown.com

Shelby Bottoms Park

2021 Fatherland St.

Nashville, TN 37206

(615) 862-8474

www.nashville.gov/parks

66 I start a lot more songs than I finish, because I realize when I get into them, they're no good. I don't throw them away; I just put them away, store them, get them out of sight. **99**—Johnny Cash

Nashville Festivals

Tomato Art Festival

Intersection of 5 Points East Nashville and Woodland St.

www.tomatoartfest.com

During the Tomato Art Festival, held in East Nashville each year, the streets are closed off so that people can walk around, duck into one of the many bars and eateries, and check out the various art galleries. There is live music, and you'll see more things decorated— and more people dressed up and acting—like ripe red tomatoes this side of Valencia, Spain . . . without the mess, of course.

The Germantown Street Festival and Oktoberfest

Seventh Ave. and Monroe St.

www.nashvilleoktoberfest.com

Live German music. Beer and more beer. Great food. A 5K run. Polka dancing. This is one of Nashville's most beloved festivals, held each October in historic Germantown. Did I forget to mention the petting zoo? Lederhosen optional.

Music City Festival and BBQ Championship

Riverfront Park and Broadway

www.musiccitybbqfestival.com

Held each August in downtown Nashville, the festival offers live music and more than a hundred barbecue pros and amateurs cooking up what they hope to be the festival's winning barbecue.

Since you will be spending a great amount of time on Music Row, the name Demonbreun will no doubt come up as a direction and meeting place many, many times over. Demonbreun (pronounced *Da-mon-bre-un*) was a French Canadian fur trader, and his claim to fame was that he was the first citizen of Nashville. Viva la . . . Well, you get the point.

Bookstores

Necessary Nashville

Book Man/Book Woman
Who are they kidding? This bookstore has a book for everybody. Their shelves are stocked with used books top to bottom. If they don't have the book you're looking for, they can order it for you.
1713 21st Ave. S.
Nashville, TN 37212
(615) 383-6555
www.bookmanbookwoman.com

Rhino Books

4918 Charlotte Pike

Nashville, TN 37209

(615) 279-8031

www.rhinobooksellers.com

Books A Million

6718 Charlotte Pike

Nashville, TN 37209

(615) 352-5036

www.booksamillion.com

Books A Million

1789 Gallatin Pike North

Nashville, TN 37115

(615) 860-3133

Barnes and Noble

515 Opry Mills Drive

Nashville, TN 37214

(615) 514-5000

www.barnesandnoble.com

❝ So long as the human spirit thrives on this planet, music in some living form will accompany and sustain it and give it expressive meaning.❞—Aaron Copland

Art Supplies

Jerry's Art-A-Rama

5361 Mount View Rd.

Antioch, TN 37013

(615) 731-5901

www.jerrysartarama.com

Museums

Frist Center for the Visual Arts

The story behind the Frist Center is just as engaging as the art that hangs on its walls. Originally a post office, the building features architecture that is classic art deco. There are guided tours that focus on how the building was designed, and special attention is given to the detail of certain themes that make up what used to be the main hall of the post office.

919 Broadway

Nashville, TN 37203

(615) 244-3340

www.fristcenter.org

Country Music Hall of Fame and Museum

The museum offers visitors a comprehensive overview of the history of country music with an impressive collection of music and music memorabilia. There's also a program called Nashville Cats, which is a series that hosts top singer-songwriters talking about their influences, background, and craft.

222 Fifth Ave. S.

Nashville, TN 37203

(615) 416-2100

www.countrymusichalloffame.com

Ryman Auditorium

The Ryman is known as "The Mother Church of Country Music." The infamous Grand Ole Opry, which called the venue its home from 1943 to 1974, still broadcasts live from the Ryman a few times each month. Over the years, performers who have played the Ryman range from Elvis Presley to Elvis Costello. The Ryman offers backstage tours each day, with an informed tour guide who walks you through not only the dressing rooms but through decades of music legends and history.

116 Fifth Ave. N.

(615) 458-8700

www.ryman.com

Performance rights organization
BMI, Music Row, Nashville.

Interview:
Bradley Collins, Director, Writer-Publisher Relations, BMI

Liam Sullivan: What do you do here at BMI?

Bradley Collins: Well, to give you an overview, BMI collects and distributes performance money to songwriters and publishers. I work with songwriters who make money or who don't but are trying to get something going with their songs. I work with songwriters from the beginning to the end of their careers, because BMI, like any PRO [performance rights organization], will be the one constant in the music career of a songwriter that doesn't change. A songwriter will have different record deals, different music publishers, different booking agents. So it's full spectrum.

LS: How do you find new songwriters and new talent for BMI?

BC: I go out pretty much every night of the week looking for songwriters to build new relationships [with] and to hang and strengthen relations with songwriters that I'm already working with.

LS: If you see a songwriter, at the Bluebird Cafe, for example, who you like, will you go up and introduce yourself to them after they're finished playing?

BC: Yes, I'll introduce myself and hand them a business card. Everyone's needs are different. Some people have a publisher in place: Maybe they have a co-writing project going on with another songwriter, or maybe they don't have anything going. So my job is to know everyone in the music business and to direct a songwriter that I think has talent in the right direction.

LS: So you'd be instrumental in helping a songwriter get a record deal.

BC: Yes, but I don't do that with everyone. If I discover a songwriter or another person in my department finds a new talent that we believe strongly about, then we'll do everything we can to help. BMI acts as an industry referral; we're kind of the first line of defense. We can introduce new talent to music publishers and record labels on Music Row, but we don't take ownership of a song. You have to be affiliated with a PRO if you want to talk to a music publisher on Music Row. It use to be that people would walk up and down Music

Row, knocking on doors, handing out their materials, CDs, etc. It no longer works that way here in Nashville, yet I still see newcomers all the time knocking on doors, trying to solicit their stuff, but that is the wrong approach—you'll get nowhere.

LS: As a songwriter can I be affiliated with BMI, ASCAP, and SEASAC?

BC: As a publisher, you can, but as a songwriter, you can only be affiliated with one PRO. When I first met Charles Kelly from Lady Antebellum, they didn't have a music publishing deal, so I worked with them one-on-one, then helped with a music publishing deal, and then worked with their management. Eventually they moved on, but, as I said, we stay active with the artist throughout their career.

LS: Tell me about the BMI showcases you have.

BC: BMI has a scheduled series every Monday night at the Mercy Lounge called 8 off 8th, which features eight bands or singer-songwriters that play three songs each. It's a great place to see new talent or singer songwriters and to network if you're new to town.

LS: Do music industry professionals attend the BMI showcases?

BC: Yes, all the time, because it allows music industry folks to see what's new what's out there, and it gives [songwriters or bands] an opportunity that otherwise wouldn't be available to them.

LS: How so?

BC: Well, think of it this way: If you're new to town and you're in a band or you're a singer-songwriter, every Monday night you have the opportunity to attend a BMI-sponsored music showcase. You can hear what other bands and songwriters are playing and how they're crafting their sound. Plus, it's a great hang where you get to meet other musicians and network. If I may, I'd like to mention that if you're a songwriter and you're planning on moving to Nashville or you're coming just for a visit, come here during Tin Pan South.

LS: Please explain.

BC: Tin Pan South is a weeklong songwriter music festival held each spring here in Nashville. It's a songwriter's paradise where over a hundred well-known songwriters perform every night at various clubs around town. It's a great way to get a sense of the layout of Nashville, see some great performances, and get a flavor of what it could be like if you moved here.

LS: When you see or meet a new songwriter, what's that conversation like?

BC: If I see a songwriter at a showcase that I like, I'll introduce myself and tell them to call me to set up a meeting. Once that happens, the first thing I do is get to know the person. I like to get a sense of who they are and what they're looking to do with their music career. Then I ask them to play a couple songs and that could be with a guitar that they bring with them or if they have a CD I'll listen to that. We also have writers' rooms here at BMI that songwriters who are BMI members can book so they can work on their songs or set up a co-writing session with another songwriter. A BMI member songwriter can set that up by calling and asking for the writer relations department here at BMI.

LS: What other services does BMI offer their members?

BC: We hold a songwriters' workshop every month here at BMI, and you can register for that on our website. Jason Blume is the host and he covers topics like hit lyric analysis, the secrets of successful demos, how to publish or self-publish your songs. It's all about educating songwriters and helping them improve their craft, so at each workshop, a songwriter has the chance to pitch one of their songs to a publisher and have it critiqued.

LS: How does a songwriter copyright his or her songs? Do you do that here at BMI?

BC: We get that question asked all the time, but that is not something BMI does. If a songwriter wants to copyright their songs, they need to register with the Library of Congress at www.loc.gov and fill out a sound recording form, and they can copyright an entire album or an individual song.

LS: Finally, how would you describe your perfect day here in Nashville?

BC: My perfect day would be if the next Garth Brooks walked into my office and convinced me that he was indeed the next Garth Brooks. [*Laughs*]

CHAPTER 4
Nashville Skyline

The Nashville skyline.

Nashville Skyline

The L&C (Life and Casualty) Tower built and completed in 1957 was once the tallest building in Tennessee. Over the years the L&C has been slowly dwarfed by some of the newer buildings to come along, one of which is the AT&T Building, affectionately referred to in Nashville as the "Batman" building, because of its resemblance to Batman's mask. Nashville's skyline has been written about in songs and was the title of one of Bob Dylan's albums back in 1969.

Architecturally, the skyline is not particularly engaging, but if you look at it from the east side of the Cumberland River, it has a charm and uniqueness all its own. Along the riverfront are the old warehouses that were used to store dry goods back in the day when riverboats were the main means of cargo transportation. Towering over the warehouses is the Nashville skyline. Getting lost in Nashville is a pretty hard thing to do, because from pretty much every vantage point you can see the skyline looming in the distance. I always like to say, "If you see the Nashville skyline in front of you, you're headed in the right direction. If it's in your rearview mirror, you've gone too far." What makes Nashville endlessly engaging, however, is its wide variety of restaurants, bars, nightlife, local music scenes, and cultural offerings. When it comes to restaurants and eating out, Nashville bends the curve and offers up more of what I would call "Southern creature-comfort American food."

In Nashville, like anywhere else in the country, there are expensive steakhouses, but you can find that kind of chain restaurant anywhere. The mission of this chapter is to guide you in the right direction to some of Nashville's most beloved local eateries, bars, cafés, and live music venues, all of which lie waiting beneath the city skyline.

> **❝ I played on three of Bob Dylan's albums. I have very pleasant memories, especially the *Nashville Skyline* album was a real fun album to do. He was in a great mood. He was glad to be in Nashville, where the musicians were very laid-back and very creative. We had a lot of fun doing that album.❞** —Charlie Daniels

Coffee Bars

Coffee bars and cafés always seem to give a city a cozy touch. Most are laid-back and inviting and are perfect spots to reflect, people watch, or catch up with a friend on a cold afternoon. As we all know, there is a fairly large coffee chain that has thousands of locations around the country and is mermaid-friendly. Therefore, the list provided here is of coffee bars and cafés unique to Nashville.

Fido

You can either sit outside along the sidewalk or slide into one of the many spacious booths that are big enough to spread out and are perfect if you plan on having a meeting or to just spend the morning working on lyrics. This is one of the many places where musicians, Music Row executives and students hang out, and it's also great for people watching. Fido serves up their own unique brand of coffees along with meals that will hit the spot at any time of the day.

1812 21st Ave.

Nashville, TN 37212

(615) 777-3436

www.bongojava.com

The Frothy Monkey

Another treasure is the Frothy Monkey. A great place to get a cup of joe and something to eat and then settle into one of their booths to write or to meet up with a friend for a midmorning chat. All of the vendors that supply the provisions for the Frothy Monkey are Tennessee businesses, so this place is like local, local.

2509 12th Ave. S.

Nashville, TN 37204

(615) 292-1808

www.frothymonkeynashville.com

> **❝ It's one thing to have talent. It's another to figure out how to use it. ❞**—Roger Miller

Other great spots to hang and get caffeinated are the following:

Bongo Java

107 S. 11th St.

Nashville, TN 37206

(615) 777-3278

www.bongojava.com

Bread and Co.

4105 Hillsboro Pike

Nashville, TN 37215

(615) 292-7323

www.breadandcompany.com

Crema

15 Hermitage Ave.

Nashville, TN 37210

(615) 255-8311

www.crema-coffee.com

Dose

3431-A Murphy Rd.

Nashville, TN 37203

(615) 457-1300

www.dosecoffeeandtea.com

Drink Haus

500 Madison St., Ste. 103

Nashville, TN 37208

(615) 255-5200

www.drinkhaus.com

Provence Breads

1210 21st Ave. S.

Nashville, TN 37212

(615) 322-8887

www.provencebreads.com

Provence Downtown

315 Deaderick St.

Nashville, TN 37201

(615) 259-7927

www.provencebreads.com

Ugly Mugs

1886 Eastland Ave.

Nashville, TN 37216

(615) 915-0675

www.uglymugsnashville.com

66 The wise musicians are those who play what they can master.99

—Duke Ellington

Breakfast

The one and only Loveless Cafe, Hwy. 100, Nashville.

Necessary Nashville

Loveless Cafe

Although the Loveless is off the beaten path, it is worth the trip for the biscuits alone. I reference the Loveless Cafe in the Road Trips section of this book because it is located about thirty-five minutes from downtown, so it's not your daily breakfast joint, but the vintage neon sign out front, which is a throwback to the 1950s roadside diner, is as inviting as ever. There is also a gift shop that sells smoked hams, T-shirts, Loveless coffee mugs, and a wide range of delicious Southern preserves.

8400 Hwy. 100
Nashville, TN 37221
(615) 646-9700
www.lovelesscafe.com

Noshville

This New York–style diner situated in Midtown just a few blocks from Music Row is the place where many music industry types and musicians all chow down in the early-morning hours. While writing this book I became a regular at Noshville and was amazed at how much networking goes on at eight o'clock in the morning over bagels, scrambled eggs, and bowls of grits. So, if you're new to town and looking for authentic diner food and a good place to schmooze, this is the place.

1918 Broadway

Nashville, TN 37203

(615) 329-6674

www.noshville.com

Pancake Pantry

Located in Hillsboro Village, this is a good place to lay down the foundation, get well fed and energized before you do your weekend chores. There is often a line outside the Pancake Pantry and I've often watched in amazement from the warmth of my car people standing in the rain and bitter cold waiting to get inside the restaurant. The griddle cakes are that good.

1796 21st Ave. S.

Nashville, TN 37212

(615) 383-9333

www.thepancakepantry.com

Pfunky Griddle

In the spirit of DIY the Pfunky Griddle allows you to make your own pancakes.

2800 Bransford Ave.

Nashville, TN 37204

(615) 298-2088

www.pfunkygriddle.com

Pied Piper

Sleep in late? Still want scrambled eggs? This is your place. Breakfast is served all day. But remember, no pj's: proper attire required.

1601 Riverside Dr.

Nashville, TN 37216

(615) 228-2795

No website, so swing on by.

Bagel Face

700 Main St.

Nashville, TN 37206

(615) 730-8840

www.bagelfacenashville.com

Honky-tonk Legends, lower
Broadway, Nashville.

Word on the Street
with Nashville Songwriter Amber Hayes

Hometown: Weleetka, OK

I met up with Amber for some breakfast at Noshville, located in Midtown, Nashville, and a stone's throw from Music Row. A couple of days later I went to see Amber perform at a live radiocast that WSM 650 AM radio hosts each month at the Station Inn.

Liam Sullivan: When did you first decide that you wanted to make music your life?

Amber Hayes: When I turned fifteen I was up for an award at a music award show that was held in Ada, Oklahoma, for local performers. The host of the awards show that night was Jean Shepard.

LS: Do you mean *the* Jean Shepard who sang the song "Tired of Playing Second Fiddle to an Old Guitar?" She's a Grand Ole Opry legend.

AH: Yep, that's the one. However, I didn't win the award but Jean came up to me afterwards and said, "I gotta tell you something, girl, I want you to come to Nashville and sing with me." A couple of weeks later Jean Shepard called my parents and said she wanted me to sing with her at Ernest Tubb's Midnite Jamboree, so we all loaded up in the van and drove to Nashville. After that I was hooked.

LS: What was your experience like when you finally decided to move and make Nashville your new home?

AH: I moved to Nashville right out of high school. I was here in town for one day and turned around and drove back home to Oklahoma. I had an apartment and a roommate but I come from a really small town so Nashville was the big city and it was kind of overwhelming. Two weeks later I got back in my car and came back and got settled into my Nashville life. I enrolled at Trevecca University here in Nashville and studied communications. But I really wanted to get out there and start performing. At that time I was doing mostly covers by artists like Reba, Shania Twain, Martina McBride. I just wanted to sing.

LS: How long after settling in here in Nashville did you start playing out and doing gigs?

AH: I didn't jump into the music scene right away; I actually started my own business, which was a workout facility for women. Around the same time, I had wanted to buy a new car, but the car salesman actually told me to save my money and to put it toward my music career. I thought that was pretty funny, a car salesman talking me out of buying a car. That doesn't happen every day. [*Laughs*] So I actually got into musical theater and took some parts, which helped me with my vocals and feeling comfortable on stage.

LS: What did you do to get your career off the ground?

AH: Well, I started writing my own songs and started attending open mic/writers' nights at places like the Commodore to improve my songwriting craft. To get a music publishing deal you have to write your own songs. I started teaming up with other people co-writing songs, and out of those sessions, we started doing some demos at a place here in Nashville called the Funhouse so we would have something for people to listen to. From those co-writing sessions came my first single, "C'mon"

LS: Tell me about the process. How did you get your song on the radio?

AH: After I decided that "C'mon" would be the single, I knew I needed management. I wanted to take my career to the next level. Because I had done musical theater, I had a proven track record as a performer to get out on stage night after night and perform. That was key to getting management to back me. I signed with a management company called FUNL here in Nashville. Soon after that, I started doing a radio station tour, doing interviews. I've done about seventy radio stops across the country while touring, so it's been a thrill.

LS: Describe your favorite Nashville moment as a musician.

AH: So far, my favorite Nashville moment was back when I was doing musical theater and got to sing on the legendary Ryman stage. It was really emotional. I love country music, and to get a chance to sing on the stage where legends like Patsy Cline and Dolly Parton have performed is something I will never forget. It was a dream come true.

LS: What advice would you give to women who are thinking of moving to Nashville?

AH: I can tell you what Barbara Mandrell told me when I had a chance to meet her: She said, "You have to remember that you are in control, you are the boss, this is a business, and you are the product and no one is going to sell it and work at it like you can." That really stuck with me, because there are always people who are looking to take advantage of you.

LS: Describe your perfect Nashville day.

AH: My perfect Nashville day would probably start out with pancakes at the Pfunky Griddle, and then after that I would head over to the Country Music Hall of Fame to check out one of their songwriter sessions. After that I would get together with some of my friends and try to write a hit song. [*Laughs*] After writing, I would probably end up at the Opry or downtown listening to some country music at the honky-tonks. I love the Tennessee Titans, so I love game day in Nashville as well.

Lunch

Hog heaven! Jack's Bar-B-Que on lower Broadway, Nashville.

Necessary Nashville

Jack's Bar-B-Que
This was the first place I had barbecue when I came to Nashville. I was sitting on the second floor with my co-worker and colleague. While we ate our lunch I looked across the street and saw the Ernest Tubb record store. I turned to my co-worker and said, "Who's Ernest Tubb?" to which he replied, "I wouldn't say that too loud in this town."

I knew virtually nothing about country music back then, but I digress. Jack's is a must, and there is nothing better than having a pulled pork sandwich with sides like mac and cheese to fuel up on before you go honky-tonking. Jack's is right in the middle of all the honky-tonks along lower Broadway, and because of its two-story layout you're always guaranteed to get a seat.
416-A Broadway
Nashville, TN 37210
(615) 254-5715
www.jacksbarbque.com

Dan McGuiness

This spacious pub, which is situated on the top of Demonbreun Street, is the place where Music Row types and musicians meet to put on the feed bag. On most weekdays the place is abuzz with Music Row gossip about who's getting a publishing deal, and inevitably there is always one table filled with hungover-looking musicians yapping about the gig they performed the night before. On Thursdays there is a fish-and-chips special, which fills the place up pretty quickly, but it's worth it. Over the years I've had multiple meetings at Dan McGuiness for business or to conduct interviews. The place has a great vibe and it's a great place to meet up with friends or to see live music, which takes place on the back patio.

1538 Demonbreun St.

Nashville, TN 37203

(615) 252-1991

www.danmcguinnesspub.com

Marche

For years the only place you could find something descent to eat in East Nashville was a place called the Fork and Spoon, which at best was a bland greasy spoon. Today East Nashville is alive with various food options, and Marche is at the top of the list. Because of this culinary renaissance, well-known musicians from all genres have flocked to Marche, making it one of the more desirable spots in town to have lunch. Who knows? Maybe Jack White will even ask you to pass the salt.

1000 Main St.

Nashville, TN 37206

(615) 262-1111

www.marcheartisanfoods.com

Elliston Place Soda Shop

Step back in time and indulge in one of the most American experiences this side of the Mississippi. Elliston Place has been in operation since 1939. Outside is the Elliston sign, which is in classic neon. Inside, you can sit at a booth and play the jukebox that has hits from the '50s. The food is straightforward burgers and french fries, but the real reason to go is for their milk shakes. You'll be happy you did.

2111 Elliston Place

Nashville, TN 37203

(615) 327-4030

Here are some more places for your consideration to lunch it up.

Blue Coast Burrito

6800 Charlotte Pike

Nashville, TN 37209

(615) 354-8171

www.bluecoastburrito.com

Burger Up

2901 12th Ave. S.

Nashville, TN 37204

(615) 279-3767

www.burger-up.com

Corner Pub

2000 Broadway

Nashville, TN 37203

(615) 327-9250

www.cornerpubtn.com

Fat Mo's

2608 Gallatin Pike

Nashville, TN 37216

(615) 226-5012

No website, so swing on by.

Pizza Perfect

1602 21st Ave. S.

Nashville, TN 37212

(615) 329-2757

www.pizzaperfectonline.com

Pizza Pie in the Sky

110 Lyle Ave.

Nashville, TN 37203

(615) 321-1223

www.pspizza.com

Rotier's

2413 Elliston Place

Nashville, TN 37203

(615) 327-9892

www.rotiers.com

SATCO

San Antonio Taco Co.

416 21st Ave. S.

Nashville, TN 37203

(615) 327-4322

www.thesatco.com

> **66 After silence, that which comes nearest to expressing the inexpressible is music. 99**
> —Aldous Huxley

Elvis keeping watch over the honky-tonks, lower Broadway, Nashville.

Meat and 3

The description says it all: One portion meat and three sides. This is a big part of the Nashville experience if there ever was one. Most places offer a different meat each day, and sometimes fish, but the choices of sides are synonymous with Southern comfort food like mac and cheese, fried okra, black-eyed peas, and turnip greens. Synonymous never tasted so good!

Arnold's Country Kitchen

605 8th Ave. S.

(615) 256-4455

Nashville, TN 37203

www.hollyeats.com

Hours: 6:00 A.M.–2:30 P.M.

Cool Café

1110 Hillsboro Rd.

Franklin, TN 37064

(615) 599-0338

www.cool-cafe.com

Copper Kettle

94 Peabody St.

Nashville, TN 37210

(615) 742-5545

www.copperkettlenashville.com

Monell's

1235 N Sixth Ave

Nashville, TN 37208

 (615) 248-4747

www.monellstn.com

Sylvan Park

4502 Murphy Rd.

Nashville, TN 37203

(615) 292-9275

www.hollyeats.com

Lunch and dinner

DIXIE DOWNTURN

Their motto is "You're Broke. We're Broke. Let's Party":
This site offers up the bestest, freest, and cheapest
things to do in Nashville.
www.dixiedownturn.com

Necessary Nashville

The Sweet Spots

Bobbie's Dairy Dip
5301 Charlotte Pike
Nashville, TN 37209
(615) 292-2112
www.bddinc.com

Sweet 16th Bakery
311 16th St. N.
Nashville, TN 37206
(615) 226-8367
www.sweet16th.com

Sweet & Sassy
604 Gallatin Rd. N.
Nashville, TN 37115
(615) 865-1450
www.snsbakery.com

Interview:
Robert Ellis Orrall, Songwriting Craft

Hometown: Boston, MA

Signed to RCA Records in the 1980s, Robert Ellis Orrall recorded three albums with producer Roger Bechirian (Elvis Costello, Squeeze) and toured with bands such as the Kinks and U2. In recent years he has written songs and produced albums for artists like Taylor Swift and Lindsay Lohan. I met up with Robert to discuss the craft of songwriting and to try and get to the bottom of one of the most mysterious question out there in the music business: "What makes a hit song a hit song"?

Liam Sullivan: How did you make your way to Nashville and what was that experience like?

Robert Ellis Orrall: I started coming to Nashville because I knew it was where songwriters lived and worked. The first week I was here, I went to a show at the Bluebird and was knocked out. I moved here three years later.

LS: Where does a song begin for you? Story, topic, melody, or lyric? What's your process?

REO: It's different every time. I try to pick up the guitar or put my hands on the piano every day. Sometimes things spill out and I can't stop until I'm done. Sometimes I have a writing session set up with an artist or band that's going into the studio, so I prepare a few ideas. Sometimes I make up a song on a walk and sing the whole thing into my iPhone I use to carry around a tape recorder. If I'm not inspired, I move on to something else.

LS: For my money when I hear the right lyric, one that speaks to me, I'm automatically drawn to that song. So when it comes to lyric writing what's your process? Do you start out with a main theme or just a few lines and build from there?

REO: Very often the first few lines pop into my head. If I'm writing for a project I'm producing, I can just say what I want the way I want to say it. Of course, I'm trying to connect my joy, heartbreak, anxiety, and euphoria to the listener, so I work at it. It's not just stream of consciousness. If I'm writing with an artist, my job is to suggest lines and ideas, then let the artist decide if it's something they would say. In those cases, I want to be invisible: I'm there to amplify the artist's emotions.

LS: Do you throw out a lot of "good" lyrics while waiting for the "right" lyric?

REO: Most of the time, they don't make it pencil-to-paper until I think it's right. But I will cross [words] out and make the lyrics better every chance I get. Sometimes I make changes in the studio, months after I thought the song was finished.

LS: What can you tell me about how a song unfolds for you?

REO: Honestly, sometimes I finish something by myself, play it the next day and don't remember how I wrote it or how it came about. I just express myself. It's like therapy in a way. Some days I write songs while I'm waiting for a co-writer to show up.

LS: How important is the way a word sounds, as opposed to its meaning?

REO: In a lot of pop and rock songs, it can be more important. Just the way the words flow can make a song stick in your head. In country songs, words need to make sense, they need to be clear, they need to be concise.

LS: What do you do when you feel blocked while trying to compose a song? Do you keep chipping away, even when it seems like nothing's coming?

REO: If nothing's coming, I do something else. Watch football, paint a painting. Then my mind wanders and I'm back to singing into my iPhone!

LS: What is the purpose of a bridge in a song?

REO: I'm a fan of bridges, but only if there is something to say that hasn't been said. I don't want a bridge for the sake of another musical section. Great solos are underrated.

LS: In collaborating, do you stick to your guns if you really believe in something, or do you stand down in the interest of keeping the process moving?

REO: I make a case for what I believe is right. If I'm writing with an artist, and it's not something they would say or a melody that doesn't fit their style, that makes the decision. But in general, if the song is great, I'm not quibbling over a few words.

LS: Do you trust your gut, even when you are getting other opinions about a song you've written?

REO: Maybe I didn't thirty years ago, but I sure as hell do now.

LS: When writing, what is your work rhythm like? Stay with it? Take breaks? Work on another song if you are having a mental block?

REO: When co-writing, I like to work in four-hour blocks, no breaks. Just dive into the pool and keep swimming. When I'm by myself I lose track of time. I can start a song at 6 A.M. and finish recording the master at midnight.

LS: If writing for someone in particular, how do you get inside the spirit of their art and offer something that will resonate with that artist?

REO: Well, my job is to reflect and amplify what the artist is all about. I get to know their music before I meet them, talk to their A&R person to hear about direction, ask the artist what's going on in their life. Sometimes the right question is just, "What kind of song haven't you done yet?"

LS: Do you always write to get a hit? Or do you ever put energy into a song that may not hit the charts but will have a meaningful place in the flow of an album?

REO: Sometimes I craft songs for the radio and sometimes I write songs that no one will hear but [that] mean everything to me. Sometimes art and commerce meet in the middle, like with "What If It's You," one of Reba [McEntire]'s hits. "Ultimate," Lindsay Lohan's end-title song in *Freaky Friday*, was written just for fun, but then it found its way to a platinum record.

LS: I know this is a loaded question, but in your opinion, what makes a song a hit? What are some of the crucial ingredients?

REO: Can't answer that one. I know the answer but won't give it up. Just kidding. If I knew the answer to that I'd write one a week, probably while sitting on the beach. [*Laughs*]

LS: Do you write every day?

REO: I try to play a little something and see what happens. My record labels, Infinity Cat and Plastic 350, keep me busy as well, but writing is my passion. It seems like every year I get to my office earlier and leave later. I love it more than ever.

LS: What advice do you have for singer-songwriters who want to come to Nashville to pursue their careers in music? What are some of the things that you have learned over the years working in the music business here in Music City?

REO: Get lucky. I've been very lucky, and I know luck is a big part of success. Of course, you have to work your ass off, live and breathe it. By doing that, you in a sense create your own luck. When a sliver of opportunity shows itself, you've gotta be ready to make the most of it. Some of the best songs I've written haven't been recorded because luck hasn't come their way yet. I don't pick the singles; the labels do. And once my single is Top Five, sometimes I get lucky, and we have a Number One party!

LS: As a songwriter working and living in Nashville, what are some of the things you love most about this town?

REO: I love the sense of community. You can show up here, go out at night, and have a half-dozen songwriter friends in a week. On the rock side, all the bands on Infinity Cat lift each other up. They go out of their way to help touring bands have a great turnout at their shows. They play on each other's records, lend equipment, wear each other's T-shirts. Community is everything.

Cheap Eats

Hungry, but your bank balance indicates that the three-course chow-down at Chez Très Cher will just have to wait? Here are some choice picks that will fill you up and still leave you with enough money to buy a new set of strings.

International Market and Restaurant

Situated near Music Row, this is a big place for Vanderbilt students to hang, and an excellent and inexpensive way to fill up on the Asian buffet. The market also sells large packages of exotic spices and ingredients, a great selection of teas and teapots, and a waving porcelain kitty to make you feel welcome.

2010 Belmont Blvd.

Nashville, TN 37212

(615) 297-4453

There's no website for the market but trust me: Go there once and you will return.

Drifters BBQ

Tucked up and away from Woodland Street in East Nashville, Drifters features live bands playing outdoors during the warmer months.

1008 Woodland St.

Nashville, TN 37206

(615) 262-2776

www.driftersnashville.com

Other great places to go for a cheap chat-and-chew are:

Calypso Café

1106 Gartland Ave.

Nashville, TN 37206

(615) 227-6133

www.calypsocafe.com

Jim N' Nick's BBQ

7004 Charlotte Pike

Nashville, TN 37209

(615) 352-5777

www.jimnnicks.com

Necessary Nashville

Prince's Hot Chicken Shack

Hot chicken, or Nashville hot chicken, is a unique Music City creation. As the description suggests, it's chicken dipped in buttermilk and breaded; then the "hot" is applied in the form of cayenne pepper and other spices. Then the chicken is fried. You can choose the level of heat you want for your bird. Prince's is one of the best places to indulge your heat-seeking hunger.

123 Ewing Drive

Nashville, TN 37207

(615) 226-9442

There is no web site. It melted.

Local Taco

4501 Murphy Rd.

Nashville, TN 37209

(615) 891-3271

www.thelocaltaco.com

Sub Stop

1701 Broadway

Nashville, TN 37203

(615) 255-6482

www.substopdeli.com

66 My songwriting and my style became more complex as I listened, learned, borrowed and stole, and put my music together. 99—Boz Scaggs

Necessary Nashville

Riverside Village

To give you some background, when I first moved to Nashville, Riverside Village consisted of a hubcap joint called "Twinky's 20-Inch Twankies," a nail salon, and a gas station. The gas station is still there, but Riverside Village now hosts a top-notch sushi restaurant, a coffee shop, a locally owned pizza place, and a great local bar called the Village Pub. I'd be remiss if I didn't mention Bailey and Cato, which serves up some of the best barbecue and soul food in Nashville. So, in a word, Riverside Village is now hip, and Mitchell's deli around lunchtime is a great place to get either a full meal or one of their creative and delicious sandwiches. You might not go to Mitchell's right away when you move to Nashville, but I promise you, at some point you or your friends will insist on going there for lunch.

Mitchell Delicatessen
1402 McGavock Pike
Nashville, TN 37216
(615) 262-9862
www.mitchelldeli.com

Also in Riverside Village:

Bailey and Cato

1307 McGavock Pike

Nashville, TN 37216

www.baileyandcatorestaurant.com

Castrillo's Pizza

1404 McGavock Pike

Nashville, TN 37216

(615) 226-2900

www.castrillos.com

Sip Café

1402 McGavock Pike, Ste. B

Nashville, TN 37216

(615) 227-1035

www.mikesicecream.com

Village Pub and Beer Garden

1308 McGavock Pike

Nashville, TN 37216

(615) 942-5880

www.riversidevillagepub.com

Watnabe Sushi

1400 McGavock Pike

Nashville, TN 37216

(615) 226-1112

www.watanabesushibar.com

The honky-tonks along lower
Broadway, Nashville.

FIRST SATURDAY ART CRAWL

On the first Saturday night of every month, art galleries in downtown Nashville open their doors and serve up Nashville's best contemporary art. This event offers a great way to meet people, other musicians and artists of all stripes, and it's free, even the wine! Afterward, head over to Puckett's on Fifth Street to check out the Volunteer String Band for a nightcap and some great bluegrass.

For more information and a list of art galleries go to: www.nashvilledowntown.com

Dinner

Rosepepper Cantina

Since the title of this book is *Making the Scene*, I've tried to pick out places that are open and friendly and that you as a musician will feel comfortable in right away. Rosepepper Cantina is just that kind of place. They serve some of the best margaritas in town and the food is fantastic. In the warmer months, there is an outdoor patio that can only be described as eclectic Zen feng shui.

1907 Eastland Ave.

Nashville, TN 37206

(615) 227-4777

www.rosepepper.com

Jackson's Bar and Bistro

Since Jackson's is smack in the middle of Hillsboro Village, it's a great place to once again meet with friends before heading out to see music. The atmosphere is trendy but not in a pretentious way. The layout is comfortable it's a great place for dinner and a great place to have brunch on the weekends. They have an impressive wine and beer list and some of the most creative cocktails in

Nashville. The food ranges from pastas to burgers to healthy salads, so there is something for everyone.

2100 21st Ave. S.

Nashville, TN 37212

(615) 385-9968

www.jacksonsbarandbistro.com

Ichiban

Musicians cannot live on hot instant noodles alone. Considering that Tennessee is landlocked, you might be a bit surprised to find sushi on this list. Oh ye of little faith! Ichiban serves up some of the best fresh sushi in town. It is located in the heart of downtown Nashville, so it's a great place to start your evening and then head out to your own gig or go watch the Grand Ole Opry at the Ryman only a few blocks away. You can either eat at the sushi bar or take advantage of one of the several intimate booths. Ah, the power of fresh seafood and sake.

109 Second Ave. N.

Nashville, TN 37201

(615) 244-7900

www.ichibanusa.com

Family Wash

Probably one of the coziest restaurants in Nashville. The great thing about the Family Wash is that it's also a music venue. The stage is tiny, but it's a great place to see live music in an intimate setting and or do your own solo gig there. The other reason to go to the Family Wash is for their traditional shepherd's pie. People from all four corners of Nashville come just for this dish, but get there early, because sometimes in the cold winter months they run out.

2038 Greenwood Ave.

Nashville, TN 37216

(615) 226-6070

www.familywash.com

CHESS PIE

As you make your way through Nashville's culinary world, you will no doubt run across a curious tartlike pie called chess pie. The name and origin of this Southern dessert staple is debatable. A simple sugar, egg, and butter concoction originating in England made its way to the southern part of the U.S. way back when outhouses were all the rage. Depending on whom you ask, the name can either be derived from "cheese pie," "chest pie" (because it was sometimes kept in a chest to keep it out of reach of little hands) or, because of its simple ingredients, "just pie" as in, nothing special. Add two tablespoons of your favorite geographical accent or dialect to taste and voilà! Chess pie!

Puckett's

Fifth and Church Sts.

Nashville, TN 37219

(615) 770-2772

www.puckettsgrocery.com

Up-and comers night every Monday; shows start at 7:00 P.M.

Rumours East

1112 Woodland St.

Nashville, TN 37206

(615) 262-5346

www.rumourseast.com

Virago

1126 McGavock St.

Nashville, TN 37203

(615) 654-1902

www.mstreetnashville.com

Sambuca

601 12th Ave. S.

Nashville, TN 37203

(615) 248-2888

www.sambucarestaurant.com

Holland House

935 W. Eastland Ave.

Nashville, TN 37206

(615) 262-4190

www.hollandhousebarandrefuge.com

Eastland Café

97 Chapel Ave.

Nashville, TN 37216

(615) 627-1088

www.eastlandcafe.com

"Wanted: Drummer for Studio Work."
Music Row, Nashville.

Vegetarian/Vegan

GoJo
415 Thompson Lane

Nashville, TN 37211

(615) 332-0710

www.gojoethio.com

Ethiopian vegetarian.

Miss Saigon Vietnamese
5849 Charlotte Pike

Nashville, TN 37209

(615) 354-1351

www.misssaigontn.com

The Smiling Elephant
Thai

2213 Eighth Ave. S.

Nashville, TN 37204

(615) 891-4488

www.thesmilingelehant.com

The Wild Cow
1896 Eastland Ave.

Nashville, TN 37206

(615) 262-2717

www.thewildcow.com

Vegetarian and vegan.

Woodlands
3415 West End Ave.

Nashville, TN 37203

(615) 463-3005

www.woodlandstennessee.com

Indian vegetarian and vegan.

Late-Night Eats

Let's face it: It's a long haul between supper and tomorrow morning's breakfast. Luckily, there is a cure for the midnight munchies, so listen up, night owls, these are for you.

Necessary Nashville

Hermitage Café
Sometimes breakfast just after midnight seems like the right choice. There are many things to love about the Hermitage Café. It's open twenty-four hours a day, the food is good and cheap, and the staff is always friendly, even at three in the morning. So if you're scratching your head after you've painted the town and are in need of a late-night greasefest, the Hermitage will hit the spot.
71 Hermitage Ave.
Nashville, TN 37210
(615) 254-8871
No website, so swing on by.

Other places to consider after you're done barking at the moon are:

Athens Family Restaurant
2526 Franklin Pike
Nashville, TN 37204
(615) 383-2848
www.athensfamilyrestaurant.com
Hours: Thurs.–Sat., 24 hours

Café Coco
210 Louise Ave.
Nashville, TN 37203
(615) 321-2626
www.cafecoco.com

The Stage honky-tonk, lower
Broadway, Nashville.

Bars

Gerst Haus

Sometimes you want to go to a place in town that doesn't remind
you that you're in that town. Make sense? When you cast a
shadow over the door handle at the Gerst you leave Nashville and
enter a Bavarian beer hall. On Friday nights they have an oompah
band complete with traditional tuba and lederhosen. It took me a
couple of years to realize that they had oompah even though the
walls are covered with flyers promoting oompah music. Yes, the
beer is that good.

301Woodland St.

Nashville, TN 37213

(615) 244-8886

www.gersthaus.com

12th Street Taproom

Truly a treasure. When I first started working in the music business down on Music Row, this place was like a second home for some very simple reasons: great food, fantastic regional beer selection, and great live music. One word can describe the Taproom— *comfortable*—and there have been plenty of times that I never felt like leaving.

2318 12th Ave. S.

Nashville, TN 37204

(615) 463-7552

www.12southtaproom.com

The Gold Rush

Equidistant from two of Nashville's best music venues, the Exit/In and the End. The Gold Rush is the place where most musicians land up before and after a gig. It is a great place to get a bite to eat or if you prefer a pre-gig and post-gig beer.

2205 Elliston Place

Nashville, TN 37203

(615) 321-1160

www.goldrushnashville.com

Other watering holes worth your patronage:

3 Crow

1024 Woodland St.

Nashville, TN 37206

(615) 262-3345

www.3crowbar.com

Hanging with the mandolins.

YAZOO BREWERY

Take a tour of the brewery and get a firsthand look at how they make those tasty suds. Tours of the brewery take place on Saturday from 2:30 P.M. to 6:30 P.M., and for the price of admission, which is $6, you get a Yazoo pint glass and a tasting of all their beers. But no dunking!
910 Division St.
Nashville, TN 37203
(615) 891-4649
www.yazoobrew.com

B. B. King

152 Second Ave. N.

Nashville, TN 37210

(615) 256-2727

www.bbkingclubs.com

Blackstone

1918 West End Ave.

Nashville, TN 37203

(615) 327-9969

www.blackstonebrewery.com

Bosco's

1805 21st Ave. S.

Nashville, TN 37212

(615) 385-0050

www.boscobeer.com

Broadway Brewhouse

1900 Broadway

Nashville, TN 37203

(615) 340-0089

www.broadwaybrewhouse.net

Dino's

411 Gallatin Pike

Nashville, TN 37206

(615) 226-8998

No website, so swing on by.

Hard to describe. Easy to love. Easy to enter. Hard to leave.

Necessary Nashville

Bobby's Idle Hour

Sometimes you stumble upon a place that truly embodies the feel and spirit of the city you're in. Bobby's Idle Hour is that kind of place. It's a no-frills bar and a Nashville landmark. Crawling around inside Bobby's on any given day are Music Row types, songwriters, singers, some singing along to the jukebox, some mumbling incoherently into their beer. As I like to say "if you haven't been to Bobby's Idle Hour you haven't been to Nashville."
1028 16th Ave. S.
Nashville, TN 37212
(615) 726-0446

Division Nashville

1907 Division St.

Nashville, TN 37212

(615) 320-3472

www.divisionnashville.com

Family Wash

2038 Greenwood Ave.

Nashville, TN 37206

615-226-6070

www.familywash.com

Flying Saucer

111 10th Ave. S., Ste. 310

Nashville, TN 37203

(615) 259-7468

www.beerknurd.com

No. 308

407 Gallatin Ave.

Nashville, TN 37206

(615) 650-7344

www.bar308.com

Red Door

1010 Forrest Ave.

Nashville, TN 37206

(615) 226-7660

www.thereddoorsaloon.com

Nightclubs

Lipstick Lounge

1400 Woodland St.

Nashville, TN 37206

(615) 226-6343

www.lipsticklounge.com

Play

1519 Church St.

Nashville, TN 37203

(615) 322-9627

www.playdancebar.com

Tribe

1517-A Church St.

Nashville, TN 37203

(615) 329-2912

www.tribenashville.com

Karaoke

Fran's Eastside Tavern

There are dive bars and then there's Fran's. Situated frighteningly close to the railroad tracks that run through East Nashville, Fran's states their mission, on their Facebook page, as being "to have a good time." If that doesn't grab you, they've probably got the cheapest beer in town and karaoke on Friday nights. Spend a night at Fran's and I swear you'll feel like you spent the evening balancing yourself on the third rail.

There is no website or even a phone number: Entering Fran's is like entering another dimension, but their Facebook page does provide a map and hours of operation.

Lonnie's Western Room

208 Printers Alley
Nashville, TN 37210
(615) 251-1122
www.lonnieswesternroom.com

Ladies and Gentlemen, the Dobros!

Interview:
Mark Lonsway, Audio Engineer, Singer-Songwriter

Hometown: Fort Wayne, IN

I met up with Mark for lunch at Sam's in Hillsboro Village, which is one of the best "hang" bars for lunch in Nashville. They offer up a great menu and spacious booths to spread out in. I met Mark years ago when we were both new to Nashville. Our mutual passion for music led to a great working relationship. We played gigs together at the honky-tonks on lower Broadway, and eventually I depended on Mark to be the audio guru and producer for a recoding that I made together with my band.

Liam Sullivan: When did you first decide to become a musician?

Mark Lonsway: I've had a fascination with music since I can remember. It started with my uncle, who used to sing and play guitar at various restaurants and bars where I grew up. Ironically, I am now primarily a singer, but the guitar was what first caught my attention. I always wanted a guitar but, like many parents, my folks thought it was just a phase. Finally, one Christmas my Father handed me a package in wrapping paper and there, there it was, my first guitar. I still get excited thinking about it. In fact, I get excited every time I get a new guitar. Anyhow, the short answer to the question is that as soon as I saw my uncle play, I knew immediately that I wanted to be a musician. The role I've played as a musician has changed course, but the initial dream is still there, and I feel fortunate that I am doing what I always dreamed of doing.

LS: What was your experience of moving to Nashville like?

ML: Surreal! I came to Nashville on a $35 plane ticket simply because it was so cheap to fly here and because I loved country music. Once

I got here, I fell in love with Nashville and knew I wanted to be here. I was living in Chicago at the time and was going back and forth between Chicago and Nashville. Unfortunately I was going through a divorce. My wife at the time moved here with me and at one point I needed to go back to Chicago to do a gig. When I came back to Nashville the apartment was cleaned out; there was a package of frozen hot dogs in the sink and a futon, but that was it. So I moved into a smoke-infested hotel room for two weeks. That was pretty rough.

LS: Sounds like the storyline of a country song! You must be a great guy.

ML: [*Laughs*] Yeah, I feel like I'm a decent guy. But sometimes relationships just fall apart. I wasn't sure what the future held for me, but everyone around me was saying "you must be present to win," meaning I had to stick it out if I wanted to have any kind of success in music. You're right: My life became a country song. I went through a divorce, was unemployed, and then started taking temp jobs at temp agencies and playing gigs out of state to make some money.

LS: How did things turn around for you?

ML: I finally landed a job at a music production company on Music Row as a sound engineer. I had some experience working in the jingle industry as a sound engineer, so the job was a good fit. Actually, things were so bad that when I got the job, I was down to a hundred dollars or so. I was that close to being completely broke. But by that time I was immersed in great music and was working with great musicians. I've lived in other big cities, but Nashville was the first real music scene I had ever encountered.

LS: What do you mean by that?

ML: I love the fact that everyone is so supportive of each other. My past experience wasn't like that; people were out for themselves and would say nice things to your face but then behind your back they'd complain that they didn't get a certain gig, or get the meeting with a music publisher over you. To be honest, it took some getting used to. Musicians here in Nashville will cheer you on and mean it. The sense that I got, when I finally got settled in, was that if one of us succeeds, we all succeed, and that's a great vibe.

LS: How did you start networking and getting to know people?

ML: I started going out to all the open mic/writers' nights and would introduce myself to songwriters that I thought were good. People were very open and friendly, and so I began to build a little network. I went to Tootsies Orchid Lounge one night and saw a guitarist whose playing I really liked, and after a few weeks we started co-writing together. You can find a lot of success here in Nashville by word of mouth. If you're a good hang and you've got good chops, you can find session work, and if you're lucky, the gigs will get bigger. That's how I got into doing session gigs that were paid. I was speaking with a drummer friend of mine one day and I said, "If you ever hear of someone who needs a solid guitar player and good high harmony singer let me know." One day he called me, and that's how I got my first touring gig with Canadian country music artist Terri Clark.

LS: Tell me about touring as a gun for hire and what life is like on the road.

ML: The first time you get on a tour bus it's a rush, but after a while you begin to realize that you're on a bus with twelve other people! [*Laughs*] I had a small sleeping bunk [and] not much privacy, so the charm of being on a tour bus can wear thin pretty quickly. To be honest, it can be boring. However, I was being paid $300 a day with a $50 per diem. So I had gone from being a guy hanging on by a thread in Nashville playing open mic nights and small gigs around town to touring and playing in front of 20,000 people with Terri Clark. So these days I've got a nice balance playing my music and working with well-known country artists.

LS: What advice would you give other musicians who are thinking of moving to Nashville?

ML: Don't badger people about writing or playing with them; it just comes off bad. If you go and make friends and try to grab a gig here or there where people can hear you, the gigs will come. People move to Nashville and immediately want to write or play with the best and start bugging them. The response will be nice and polite, but it will probably also still be a no. The biggest secret is that at a certain point it doesn't matter how good you are; it's all about being a good hang. Be cool, make friends, do favors. People like to work with their friends and those they can count on. And if you still don't get the gig, at least you got a friend out of it. Win-win.

LS: Describe your favorite Nashville moment as a musician.

ML: My favorite Nashville moment didn't actually happen in Nashville, but I guess you could say it happened because I had moved to Nashville and networked my tail off. I was performing with Terri Clark and we got the chance to open up for Kenny Chesney in Wisconsin. It was a music festival and we were on the bill with Kenny, Joe Nichols, and several others. What made it a big deal was that there were 70,000 fans there, by far the largest crowd I've ever played in front of. On that tour the average crowd size was anywhere from 15,000 to 20,000, not too shabby. But 70,000 people—I felt like I had arrived, and, like I said, maybe not in Nashville, but because of Nashville.

LS: Describe your perfect Nashville day.

ML: The perfect day for me is always in the studio. I love performing live, but the studio is where the real art gets created and you can take your time and make it the way you really want it. For me, vocals are the biggest deal, so creating and capturing something great is the biggest rush, especially mixing it. Total ear candy.

CHAPTER 5

Gigging Out: Open Mic/Writer's Nights

> **❝ The best compliment I ever had is, one day I was in Nashville, some disc jockey said, 'Hey, that sounds like a Tom T. Hall song.' Up until then there hadn't been any such thing. ❞**
> —Tom T. Hall

Playing Out

O ne of the best things you can do as a musician when you first get to Nashville is to get out to some of the open mic/writers' nights that are held throughout Nashville each week. They're a great place to network and meet other musicians, but they also give you the opportunity to hear other songwriters perform. These open mic/writers' nights are very laid-back, so starting a conversation or approaching one of the singers performing after his or her set is a great way to build a network. The other advantage is that you can sign up to get up on stage and play your own songs. Each venue varies; some require that you get there early and sign in on a sheet, and others require you sign up earlier in the day. Either way, if your goal is to meet other musicians and songwriters, and or if you want to perform new material in front of a live crowd, then attending an open mic/writers' night each week is in your best interest. The open mic/writers' nights are also a great way to find a co-writer, someone you can sit down with outside of the open mic/writers' night, and write songs with. You might encounter a songwriter who writes great lyrics or a performer who has a knack for melodic hooks. So bring a business card and introduce yourself after they are done playing. Social networking online is a great tool, but as musicians, we need to be out and about, putting our best foot and song forward.

For this chapter, I interviewed Debi Champion, who runs one of the most successful open mic/writers' nights in town, and she shares her tips on how to make the most of it. Networking and having a thorough knowledge of how Nashville works will help you further your passion. The more tools you have at your disposal, the better off you'll be as you set off down the path to success.

Singer-songwriter, Nashville.

Interview:
Debi Champion, Nashville's Leading Open Mic/Writers' Night Host

One of the most popular writers' nights is held at the Commodore Grille at the Hilton Hotel down on West End Avenue. When I first heard that the writers' night was held in a hotel restaurant, I had my reservations. Hotel restaurants can be sterile and lifeless, but this space has a great vibe, the bar is alive with industry people and musicians, and the layout is nothing short of perfect. The stage is large and well lit and the sound system is great. On the night I was there, Texas native and Grammy-nominated country music hit maker David Lee performed. Lee has written some of the biggest country music hits in the past decade, including "Lucky Man," recorded by Montgomery Gentry; "I Need You," recorded by Tim McGraw and Faith Hill; and "I Want to Feel Somethin'," recorded by Trace Adkins.

The woman who hosts the writers' night at the Commodore, Debi Champion, is one of the most approachable and lovely individuals you will ever want to meet. I sat down with Debi one night at the Commodore before the evening got started to discuss her writers' night and to get her insight on what musicians can gain from spending a night at the Commodore.

Liam Sullivan: When did you first start hosting the open mic/ writers' night here at the Commodore?

Debi Champion: I've been here at the Commodore for seven years. But I've been hosting writers' night for eighteen years. At first I started out playing open mic/writers' nights doing my own material, but one night I was asked by Jack Scott, who now hosts a writers' night of his own here in Nashville at the Hotel Indigo, to host and to introduce writers to come up on stage and perform. Seemed easy enough.

LS: You obviously took to hosting writers' nights. What was it about hosting that got you hooked?

DC: Well, I couldn't live off my song royalties [*laughs*] but it was the people and songwriters that I knew that made the difference. It was a great way to hang out and support my friends and to listen to what other people were up to musically. It was a great way to work and to be out and about. I remember the first time I played by myself at an open mic/writers' night years ago and how scared I was. I didn't really know anybody. So what I try and bring to hosting is to make people playing feel welcome and make it a good experience for them and try and put them on that right road.

LS: How do you find people to play your writers' nights? Because I've noticed that you have a nice blending of successful musicians, as well as songwriters looking to get established?

DC: When I first started out, I invited friends who I had met when I was doing demo and session work down on Music Row, and from there the circle grew and the word got out.

LS: After all these years, how do you keep the writers' night fresh?

DC: Well, people who first come to Nashville are always looking for a place to get out and play their material. So there are always new faces, and the open mic/writers' night gives them that chance. The best thing about these nights, though, is that it gives you as a songwriter exposure. On any given night we have music publishers, producers, and people who are looking for a co-writer in the audience. It's just a great place to network.

LS: What are some of the other benefits?

DC: Well, you know, to a large extent this town works by word of mouth. So you can test your songs out in front of other people who are doing the same thing. By listening to other performers, you can watch and learn. You can see what they're doing and decide what you like and don't like. Sometimes you can learn more by watching and listening at a writers' night than [by] actually playing.

LS: How can songwriters sign up to play your writers' night?

DC: Come to the Commodore on any Tuesday, Wednesday, Thursday, or Sunday night and sign up with me any time before 9:00 P.M. and I'll get you up there. Everybody does it that way the first time; it's like a live audition. Here in Nashville you have to jump right into it.

LS: How many songs can a songwriter play?

DC: Usually one or two depending how I'm doing on time. Some nights there are ten to fifteen people who sign up and other nights only three or four sign up.

LS: How have things changed in terms of hosting an open mic/ writers' night in the past eighteen years?

DC: Well, when I first started playing gigs, my husband was out of work and I would play for tips playing at a place called Gillies to make ends meet. Back then Kenny Chesney would come up on stage and sit in with me. So that's changed. [*Laughs*]

LS: Oh, is he big now?

DC: Who? Kenny Chesney? [*We both laugh*] Yeah, he's pretty big. [*Smiles*] But to be honest, now all you see is Chesney's big show and all the success he's had, but back then, when he was starting out, he worked real hard at his craft and would play every chance he got.

LS: What's your favorite thing about Nashville?

DC: Kayaking. [*Laughs*] Seriously, it has to be the music, and of course all the great people I've met over the years. There's a great community of musicians in this town, and sometimes having lots of friends is more important than selling lots of albums.

LS: But wouldn't it be nice to have both?

DC: Absolutely!

. . . And with that, Debi made her way to the mixing board to check levels and arrange the microphones on stage for that night's open mic/writers' night.

Julie Forester playing her
heart out, Nashville.

**66 You're gonna have to learn
to get out there in front of those
cameras and hold your head
up. Take charge when you're
singing. 99**—Patsy Cline

Debi's Tips: Making the Most of an Open Mic/Writers' Night

- Check in with the host of the writers' night thirty minutes before you're scheduled to play, to let the host know that you are still there and ready to play.

- Make sure your guitar is tuned and that you're ready to get on stage when your name is called.

- Keep whatever song you sing three to three and a half minutes long.

- Don't make the introduction to your song longer than the song itself. There are other songwriters waiting to perform, so be considerate.

- If you can't make a writers' night, let the host know ASAP. Try and give them as much notice as possible so they can find a replacement for your slot.

Why You Should Play and Attend an Open Mic/Writers' Night

These evenings are great for all musicians, from sax players to drummers. This is a great place to meet other musicians and singer-songwriters, make new friends, and find a co-writing partner and or get into a band situation.

- You can gain exposure. These nights give people a chance to hear your songs and see how you perform live on stage.

- There are always music industry people in the crowd looking for new talent.

- It's a good way to get some demo work and gigs, and to meet other songwriters for co-writing opportunities.

- You can try out new material and get a reaction from a live audience.

- It's a great way to keep your chops up and to know what's going on in the music business down on Music Row.

Open Mic/Writers' Night Venues

Douglas Corner Café

Every Tuesday night is open mic night, which is a great way to either participate or sit back and listen to what other musicians and singer-songwriters are up to. To sign up call (615) 292-2530 between 1:00 P.M. and 6:00 P.M. on the Tuesday that you wish to perform. Each performer gets to play two songs. So bring your A game.

2106 Eighth Ave. S.

Nashville, TN 37204

(615) 298-1688

www.douglascorner.com

Commodore Grille

Hilton Hotel

2613 West End Ave.

Nashville, TN 37203

(615) 327-4707

www.commodoregrille.com

Puckett's

Fifth and Church Sts.

Nashville, TN 37219

(615) 770-2772

www.puckettsgrocery.com

Nashville landmark, Hatch Show Print, lower Broadway, Nashville.

HATCH SHOW PRINT

In business making promotional posters for concerts and artists since 1879, Hatch Show Print is a great place to order a custom-designed poster for your gig or to buy posters that are for sale to hang on the walls of your new place.
316 Broadway
(615) 256-2805
www.hatchshowprint.com

Bluebird Cafe

4104 Hillsboro Pike

Nashville, TN 37215

(615) 383-1461

www.bluebirdcafe.com

Café Coco

210 Louise Ave.

Nashville, TN 37203

(615) 321-2626

www.cafecoco.com

QUICK TIP

Oftentimes you'll meet people and they will ask you, "Who are some of your influences musically?" Best advice is to have three artists in mind at all times and leave it at that. The other thing people will ask you is, "Who do you sound like?" I never liked this question because I always get so caught up in trying to think of who I sound like that the answer falls flat and the response is usually a tepid "Oh, okay, cool." Again, put some thought into this answer. Think of three artists that you genuinely think you sound like and leave it at that. Memorize your answers to these questions and remember: Less is more, be specific, and don't ramble.

Listening Room

209 10th Ave. S.

Nashville, TN 37203

(615) 259-3600

www.listeningroomcafe.com

Red Rooster

1530 Demonbreun St.

Nashville, TN 37203

(615) 457-2781

www.nashvillerooster.com

12th and Porter

114 12th Ave. N.

Nashville, TN 37203

(615) 320-3754

www.12thandporterlive.com

> There's an old saying in the music business regarding songwriters being influenced by other songwriters, and it goes something like this: "Amateurs borrow, professionals steal." Be a pro.

Hall of Fame Lounge

Best Western Hotel

1407 Division St.

Nashville, TN 37203

(615) 256-4255

There's no web site, so swing on by.

Hotel Indigo

301 Union St.

Nashville, TN 37201

(615) 891-6000

www.writerartist.com

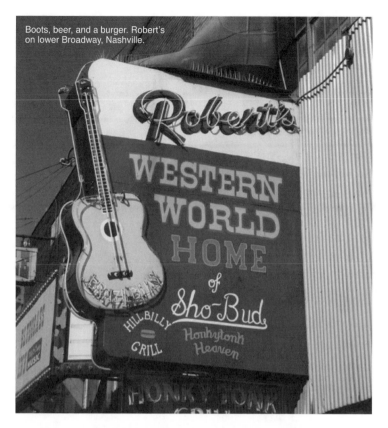

Boots, beer, and a burger. Robert's on lower Broadway, Nashville.

Live Music Venues

Heading out to see live music in Nashville is the best way to embrace this city and the diversity of music it offers. A great place to start is along lower Broadway in downtown. This is where all the honky-tonk bars are. Standing in the shadows of the Ryman Auditorium, these bars give off a vibe that is uniquely Nashville. The crowds are a mixture of tourists and locals, as well as musicians trying to get noticed. However, more often than not, country cover bands play and are open to requests. I have found visiting Nashville's music venues to be a great education in terms of getting a sense of the history of Nashville. On any given evening you can walk down lower Broadway, where the air is filled with an undisguisable cacophony of music spilling out of all the bars. The energy is infectious, and you can wander in and out of each bar, checking out different bands, having a beer, and then moving on to the next. There is no cover charge, but after most sets a tip jar is passed around for the band's efforts.

Honky-Tonk, Country, Bluegrass

Tootsies Orchid Lounge

Tootsies is the queen of the honky-tonks. A great place to hang your hat for an afternoon and watch local musicians play country music hits from Hank Williams to Garth Brooks.

422 Broadway

(615) 726-0463

www.tootsies.net

Roberts Western World

At Roberts you can get a burger, a beer, and a pair of boots, all while listening to some of the best live country music cover bands on lower Broadway.

416 Broadway

Nashville, TN 37203

(615) 244-9552

www.robertswesternworld.com

Other places to see live music in downtown Nashville include:

Bluegrass Inn

418 Broadway

Nashville, TN 37203

(615) 726-2799

www.laylasbluegrassinn.com

Douglas Corner

2106 Eighth Ave. S.

Nashville, TN 37204

(615) 298-1688

www.douglascorner.com

Legends

428 Broadway

Nashville, TN 37203

(615) 248-6334

www.legendscorner.com

Second Fiddle

420 Broadway

Nashville, TN 37203

(615) 248-4818

www.thesecondfiddle.com

The Stage

412 Broadway

Nashville, TN 37203

(615) 726-0504

www.thestageonbroadway.com

Station Inn

402 12th Ave. S.

Nashville, TN 37203

(615) 255-3307

www.stationinn.com

The 5 Spot music venue,
East Nashville.

Rock/Indie Rock

The End

Not sure what your definition of the word *rustic* is, but the End is basically a building with four walls a stage and a bar. When the lights are turned up, the interior can be rather scary. Regardless, this a great place to play an entry-level gig and to work out the snags in your set.

2219 Elliston Pl.

Nashville, TN 37203

(615) 321-4457

www.myspace.com/theendnashville

Exit/In

The Exit/In has been Nashville's leading rock club since the early 1970s. Everyone from the Police to Bill Monroe has played there. National acts still play there when they come through town, so it's a good place to see your favorite band or artist up close.

2208 Elliston Place

Nashville, TN 37203

(615) 321-3340

www.exitin.com

The 5 Spot

This venue has live music pretty much every night of the week. On Wednesday they host an evening called Old-Time Jam, which recalls an earlier time, when country songwriters would sit around picking together. Things are laid-back and the place is filled with musicians with varying backgrounds.

1006 Forrest Ave.

Nashville, TN 37206

(615) 650-9333

www.the5spotlive.com

FooBar

They have two stages at FooBar for bands to play on: One is smoking and the other, which requires walking through a door, is nonsmoking. The crowd is young and hip and the atmosphere is a strange blend of cool rock dive bar and a VFW hall.

2511 Gallatin Ave.

Nashville, TN 37206

(615) 226-7305

www.thefoobarnashville.com

French Quarter Café

The French Quarter has one of the best stages to play in East Nashville. The venue is very band- and singer-songwriter-friendly. It's a great place to book a gig and play your songs in front of a live audience. There's always a good-size crowd of locals, who, if they like what they hear, will put their hands together and clap. If they don't, then a monkey in a beret wearing an ascot and smoking a cigarette will come out and hit you on the head with a loaf of bread.

823 Woodland St.

Nashville, TN 37206

(615) 227-3100

www.frenchquartercafe.com

Mercy Lounge/Cannery Ballroom

One of the more prime live music venues in Nashville. Everyone from Emmylou Harris to Muse and the White Stripes has played here. It's also a great place to meet and mingle with other musicians. Why? Because the place is swarming with them!

One Cannery Row

Nashville, TN 37203

(615) 251-3020

www.mercylounge.com

Other places to check out if you like it loud:

3rd & Lindsley

818 Third Ave. S.

Nashville, TN 37210

(615) 259-9891

www.3rdandlindsley.com

The Basement

1604 Eighth Ave. S.

Nashville, TN 37203

(615) 254-8006

www.thebasementnashville.com

The Rutledge

410 Fourth Ave. S.

Nashville, TN 37210

(615) 782-6858

www.therutledgelmv.com

ERNEST TUBB MIDNITE JAMBOREE

After the *Grand Ole Opry, Ernest Tubb Midnite Jamboree* is the second-longest-running radio program in America. Broadcast live every Saturday night from the Texas Troubadour Theater in Music Valley, the *Jamboree* offers a great opportunity to see acts perform live in a small intimate setting and to be part of a live radio audience. For more information, go to www.etrecordshop or visit the Texas Troubadour Theater at 2416 Music Valley Drive, Nashville, TN 37214, or call (615) 889-2474.

Printers Alley

Printers Alley, downtown Nashville.

This small alley situated between Third and Fourth Avenues in downtown Nashville has played a big part in the city's history. Originally the center of printing press companies in the 1940s and '50s, it later became a red-light district of sorts for Nashville, filled with exotic dance clubs for gentlemen. In the 1960s country singers such as Chet Atkins and Waylon Jennings performed in various clubs there. Today the alley is alive and well, with live music being offered up every night.

Bourbon Street Blues and Boogie Bar

220 Printers Alley

Nashville, TN 37210

(615) 242-5837

www.bourbonstreetblues.com

Fiddle and Steel Guitar Bar

210 Printers Alley

Nashville, TN 37210

(615) 251-9002

www.fiddleandsteel.com

Lonnie's Western Room

208 Printers Alley

Nashville, TN 37210

(615) 251-1122

www.lonnieswesternroom.com

Interview:
Joe Limardi, Program Director, WSM 650 AM

Hometown: Pittsfield, MA

For the last eighty-five years, WSM 650 AM has played a significant role in shaping the musical landscape of Nashville. It was on a Saturday back in October 1925 that WSM aired for the first time.

Today WSM plays an all-country format embracing the history of country music and broadcasts the *Grand Ole Opry* live every Tuesday, Friday, and Saturday night. Expanding the format to include a wider range of bluegrass and Americana was the brainchild of the WSM's program director, Joe Limardi. I met up with Joe one afternoon at the WSM offices, located at the Gaylord Opryland hotel, where WSM is headquartered.

Liam Sullivan: Where are you from originally, and how did you become the program director for WSM 650 AM?

Joe Limardi: I grew up in Pittsfield, Massachusetts, which is located in the far western corner of the state. After college I moved to Boston and got into radio, and I began to work in different markets in the northeast as a DJ. After about five years of doing that, I got the opportunity to be a program director at a failing AM station, WSUB, in Groton, Connecticut, which is the submarine-manufacturing capital of the world. WSUB's format at the time was playing standards, but the powers that be wanted to change it to an all-talk format. After two years of doing that, I took a job in New Bedford, Massachusetts, but I didn't want to be an on-air host. I had dreams of becoming a general manager for a radio station, but I knew that in order to do that, I had to have radio sales experience. So I took a job at a radio station in New Bedford in sales and I hated it, but it was a necessary evil because I knew that I needed to learn all aspects of the business, which is a good piece of advice: Whether you want to be in radio or if it's your dream to be a singer-songwriter, you have to know how the business works.

LS: So you went from a submarine town to an old whaling town in New Bedford?

JL: [*Laughs*] Yeah, that's one way to look at it. I was keeping my career coastal. One day I got a call from the general manager offering me the job of promotions director, which allowed me to learn that side of the trade, and I did some crazy promotional things to build our listenership.

LS: I have to ask. What were some of those crazy things?

JL: Well, I guess the craziest thing I did to build listenership was I lived on the roof of a Dunkin' Donuts for a week.

LS: [*Laughs*] Who hasn't! You lived on the roof of a Dunkin' Donuts for a week? Did they at least give you free donuts and coffee?

JL: [*Laughs*] Well, it was great promotion for them and [for] the radio station I was working at. It was located at a busy intersection, and I lived in a tent on the roof. The strange thing about that whole experience was that I was also a spokesperson for Nutrisystem's weight loss program, at the time so I couldn't go off the weight loss program diet. So Nutrisystem would swing by with food and I would lower a small basket from the roof and they would put my food in that and I would hoist it back up. But it was brutal because my tent was next to one of the main exhaust vents on the roof, so I smelled every old-fashioned that Dunkin' Donuts made, but I had to resist. Besides quick bathroom breaks and the occasional shower, I was up on the roof for a week. With the great publicity and exposure that that stint generated, they eventually made me the program director.

LS: How did you finally make your way to Nashville and become the program director for WSM?

JL: I was working for Cumulus radio and I was moving around a lot, working at different stations and trying to advance my career, and I landed up here in Nashville in 2004, working at one of the Cumulus radio stations and I just loved this city. But my contract ran out, and although I didn't want to leave Nashville, I had to go where the job was. I took a job offer in New York, but all the while I wanted to get back to Nashville.

LS: What was it about Nashville that you loved?

JL: Nashville had a lot of the things that I love about the South. There's a diversity of people who come from different parts of the country to make Nashville their new home. The people you meet here greet you with a smile, they look you in the eye, and everyone seems to have another job, whether that's painting or whatever, and it isn't cutthroat like other cities. Everyone is doing something creative and we all work together and support each other. It's also an easy place to live: It's laid-back and affordable and the winters are short, a lot less extreme compared to living up North. [*Laughs*] So I was up in New York working at a radio station in Poughkeepsie and I got a call from WSM. At that time I really didn't know anything about the station. I knew that WSM aired the *Grand Ole Opry* and was a country music radio station, but beyond that I knew precious little. Oddly enough, that was exactly the kind of program director that they were looking for, so I took the job. They didn't want to be the old radio station that everyone had come to know; they wanted it to be the next generation of WSM. So my job was to preserve the heritage but at the same time give it some new life. We've done that by surrounding that classic sound with cool music from the world of bluegrass and Americana. So it just all fit together. We take our listeners on a musical journey every day, and we give them a taste of everything that is country music in terms of what was, what is, and what it's going to be. That's our mission, to build on that tremendous music history as a radio station but to also embrace a new audience of musicians and country music lovers.

LS: How does WSM embrace the new singer-songwriters coming to Nashville?

JL: Come out and see us and our DJs, whether it's at the live broadcasts we do at the Station Inn or at Bluegrass Underground at the Volcano Room. All of us here at WSM are open to young singer-songwriters; we're always willing to shake a hand and hear what musicians have to say. We never turn anyone away, because we remember that's what this station was all about, so why wouldn't we be like that today? That's how Loretta Lynn did it years ago: She went to a radio station with her record and they gave her a chance, and that's who we are at WSM. We're open to everyone.

LS: In your time here at WSM and in Nashville, for that matter, what was that one moment that you're most proud of?

JL: It had to be back in May 2010, when we were flooded out of the Gaylord Opryland and we stayed on the air. There was not one second that we went off the air. We were there for our listeners and informing them of what was going on with the floods. After eighty-five years, we were still on the air, and even though we had to pack everything up from here and bring the show back down to the original transmission tower in Brentwood, which has stood there since 1932, we plugged into the board setup a foldout table with a pair of headphones and kept broadcasting. Making sure that this iconic radio station WSM stayed on the air, we had to stop playing music for a while to make sure that our listeners were okay, but no matter how bad the floods were, we stayed right with them and on air.

TENNESSEE JAZZ AND BLUES SOCIETY

If you need a break from country music, which is pervasive throughout Nashville, and want to dive headfirst into something a little different, contact the following. They have an open blues jam on Tuesday nights, along with a slew of other live concerts and events.

P.O. Box 121293
Nashville, TN 37212
(615) 975-5610
www.jazzblues.org

Joey McKenzie at the
Station Inn, Nashville.

Jazz

F. Scott's Restaurant and Jazz Bar

F. Scott's is a must for any jazz enthusiast. They have music six nights a week and serve up a great menu. There is never a cover.

2210 Crestmoor Rd.

Nashville, TN 37215

(615) 269-5861

www.fscotts.com

Classical

Schermerhorn Symphony Center

One Symphony Pl.

Nashville, TN 37201

(615) 687-6500

www.nashvillesymphony.org

Nashville Social Networking

365 Things to Do in Nashville

Fun Happenings

The Music Gardener

Nashville Cream

Nashvillest

Nashville Facebook

The Nashville I Wish I knew

Nashville Music Blogs

Nashville Twitter

Interview:
Amy Kurland, Founder, Bluebird Cafe

In 1982 Amy Kurland opened up the Bluebird Cafe so that musician friends of hers could have a place to go and play their songs in a setting that offered the perfect blend of great food and music. I sat down with Amy at one of Nashville's best cafés, Bread & Co., down on Hillsboro road, right across the street from the Bluebird, to talk about Amy's career and how the Bluebird Cafe became an important landmark for singer-songwriters in Nashville.

Liam Sullivan: How did the idea for the Bluebird Cafe come about?

Amy Kurland: I had gone to college for prelaw but I soon realized that that was not for me. I finally graduated with an English degree but, like all twenty-year-old kids, I had my vices, one of which was music and guys who played guitar. [*Laughs*] Back in the day, the restaurant scene here in Nashville wasn't that great, so I wanted to open a place that served great food during the day and that had great live music at night. I didn't have much of a business background, so I took some classes at a local community college here in Nashville to learn management, marketing, advertising, and the basics of running a small business.

LS: When did you open the Bluebird Cafe?

AK: I opened the Bluebird in June of 1982. I was busy running the business side of the Bluebird, so I hired someone to book the bands. It wasn't long after that that I discovered an old Nashville tradition called a "writers' night." So I thought, "Sure, why not?" Well, the night I had my first writers' night I walked into the Bluebird, and the place was packed but dead silent. The music was wonderful and at the end of the night when I rang out the cash register it was the most money the club had ever made. So I said to myself, "Writers' nights! I want this to be a writers' night club!" [*Laughs*] The music really fit the venue and really, by sheer luck, I had embraced the one thing that Nashville is all about, the song. Songs are the crowing jewels in this town.

LS: What kind of music did you have at the club before you did the writers' night?

AK: I had rock bands, jazz bands, all kinds of bands, but often people would come to the club and would complain that it was too loud. With the writers' night, it was the right sound for the room, and I grew to appreciate and connect with songwriters. I am a song person: I love lyrics. I was raised on Broadway show tunes and I think that Broadway show tunes and country songs are first cousins.

LS: How so?

AK: Because both are all about the lyrics, it's the most important element, and then the music is there to support the lyric. However, don't think for a second that country music is the poor second cousin of the Broadway tune, because the quality of the lyric and the quality of the music in country is as good as any Broadway show tune out there. That's still true today.

LS: How have the writers' nights changed at the Bluebird since that night back in 1982?

AK: Well, we began to have open mic nights as well, which allowed anyone who just got off the bus or had been in Nashville for five minutes to get up on stage and play two songs. Didn't matter— everyone was treated with tremendous care, maybe not with respect, mind you, because some performances were better than others, but definitely with care by the audience and other songwriters. There wasn't that kind of "we want you to fail" atmosphere; everyone was encouraged, and that's still the way it is today—everybody wants you to become a better songwriter.

LS: How else has it changed?

AK: Well, as the writers' nights grew, the demand to play also grew. At that time, most music venues would start their shows at 9:00 P.M., but I wanted to fill my club from six to nine. With the growing demand to play, I figured there needed to be a place for songwriters who didn't have a following but still needed exposure. Back in the day, if you wanted music industry people to come out to your showcase, you would have to spend a lot of money getting a venue, so I thought the better way to go would be to offer an early-evening writers' night that would allow music industry types to leave work and swing by the Bluebird to hear the talent we selected for the showcase. This way I could fill my club, which drove in revenue, and the songwriters could play their music for people in the industry, all before 9:00 P.M.

LS: Tell me about what happens on Sunday nights here at the Bluebird?

AK: On Sunday we have what's called open auditions for songwriters, which is sometimes a nicer setting, because there are lots of tourists, so you're playing in front of strangers and not your friends, so you get *real* feedback. It's a true Nashville experience, because if you're going to move to Nashville, it's not you against Music Row: It's all about you becoming part of the music community here. The people you meet at the open auditions at the Bluebird could be your next girlfriend or boyfriend other songwriters who you can co-write with, people who you'll land up sharing Thanksgiving dinner with. Some people grow and become better songwriters, and others find their way into the music business.

LS: How did the Bluebird Cafe become famous?

AK: Back in 1987 a few songwriter friends of mine came up with an idea to reconfigure the space at the Bluebird. The whole idea was to have music in the round, so we took all the tables and chairs and moved them around so that the songwriters would sit in a circle, not on the stage, and play for the audience. It was more intimate and the crowds who came to see music performed in the round became larger and larger. Pretty soon every singer-songwriter, famous and not so famous, wanted to play in the round at the Bluebird. That got the attention of the music industry folks, and they started coming to the Bluebird. From there, songwriters like Steve Earle, Garth Brooks, and Trisha Yearwood all got record deals by playing the Bluebird Cafe, and that's what really put the club on the map.

LS: What advice would you give a songwriter who is thinking of coming to Nashville today?

AK: I think the first step would be to go to the PROs—ASCAP, BMI, and SESAC–because they will meet with you and listen to your music and make some suggestions. I would go to the musicians' union, because they will try and sign you up, but they also have a jobs board and postings for musicians. Corner Music down on Twelfth Avenue South is another great place they have postings for musicians and people who are looking for co-writing partners, and of course check out Craigslist. But remember, you're here to build your own community of friends with other musicians, and for that kind of experience, I can't think of a better place to go than the Bluebird Cafe. Swing by for an evening! [*Laughs*]

LS: I had a feeling you were going to say that.

CHAPTER 6
Musician's Corner

Musica by Alan LeQuire.
Music Row, Nashville.

Music Row is the heart of the music industry in Nashville. Located along Sixteenth and Seventeenth Avenues, it is home to recording studios, music production and publishing companies, record labels, and the performance rights organizations (PROs). If you're a singer-songwriter, these two streets will become your second home, and from within some of the most unassuming buildings, hit records, and new careers are being launched. There is no doubt that you will find yourself coming to this part of town to either look for a job, pitch your songs, or attend one of the many outdoor music events held in the early spring and summer. As with anything in life, however, the more prepared you are for any endeavor, the better equipped you'll be to face the challenges, especially when it comes to breaking into the music market here in Nashville. The creation of Music Row is often credited to Owen Bradley, who was the music director for WSM 650 AM radio back in late 1940s. In 1954 he built a recording studio along Seventeenth Avenue South, and it was there that Patsy Cline recorded one of country music's most popular songs, "I Fall to Pieces." Since then, Music Row has launched hundreds of music careers and chart-topping music hits.

CHECKLIST FOR MUSICIANS

Bio, CD, business card, social networking profile, website, headshot. No one is going to take the time to figure out who you are. You have to come to town with a defined notion of who you are and what your music says about you. The more defined you are, the more likely it is that music industry professionals will be able to understand and help and know how they can work with you. You're also a professional, so demonstrate who your demographic or target audience is and why your music would be a perfect fit for that age group. Remember, this is a business, and the bottom line is the bottom line, so you have to show everyone you come in contact with how you can achieve. Otherwise you'll be lumped in with other musicians and songwriters who don't know what they're doing. You don't want to be in that category. As Van Morrison once said, "Music is spiritual; the music business is not."

Succeed

One of the things that is vital to your music career is that you have a basic understanding of certain music publishing terms. In any business, information is power, so as we begin this chapter, I will list some of the most important music publishing terms with an easy-to-understand definition. I've also interviewed a music publisher who hopefully will fill in some of the blanks. There is also my interview with ASCAP's vice president, Ralph Murphy, who speaks about the craft of songwriting and what key elements are important to writing a hit song.

> **QUICK TIP**
>
> Make it easy for people to work with you. Do your homework. Have a focus. Write out a business plan that is sound and makes sense. If you do that, your chances of moving your music career further along are a lot better.

PROs (Performance Rights Organizations)

ASCAP, BMI, and SESAC are PROs. They provide all sorts of help for songwriters, the most important being collecting money and sending artists checks once their songs hit the big time. Here are the listings for the PROs in Nashville and their other offices around the country.

ASCAP (American Society of Composers, Authors, and Publishers)
Nashville
2 Music Sq. W.
Nashville, TN 37203
(615) 742-5000
www.ascap.com

ASCAP Atlanta
950 Joseph E. Lowery Blvd. N.W., Ste. 23
Atlanta, GA 30318
(404) 686-8699

ASCAP Los Angeles

7920 W. Sunset Blvd., 3rd Fl.

Los Angeles, CA 90046

(323) 883-1049

ASCAP Miami

1691 Michigan Ave., Ste 350

Miami, FL 33139

(305) 673-5148

ASCAP New York

One Lincoln Plaza

New York, NY 10023

(212) 621-6000

BMI (Broadcast Music Inc.)
Nashville

10 Music Sq. E.

Nashville, TN 37203

(615) 401-2000

www.bmi.com

BMI Atlanta

3340 Peachtree Rd. N.E., Ste. 570

Atlanta, GA 30326

(404) 261-5151

BMI Los Angeles

8730 Sunset Blvd., 3rd Fl.

West Hollywood, CA 90069

(310) 659-9109

BMI Miami

5201 Blue Lagoon Dr., Ste. 310

Miami, FL 33126

(305) 266-3636

BMI New York

320 W. 57th St.

New York, NY 10019

(212) 586-2000

SESAC (Society of European Stage Authors and Composers)
Nashville

55 Music Sq. E.

Nashville, TN 37203

(615) 320-0055

www.sesac.com

SESAC Los Angeles

501 Santa Monica Blvd., Ste. 450

Santa Monica, CA 90401

(310) 393-9671

SESAC Miami

420 Lincoln Road, Ste. 502

Miami, FL 33139

(305) 534-7500

66 I didn't really know what I was doing when I started. I just started writing songs. After two songs I just continued to explore it. 99—Neil Young

Nashville Musicians Association

The NMA represents musicians, bands, composers, and vocalists. They can help with negotiating contracts, track usage of songs according to union rules, and provide a whole host of other resources for songwriters who are already established or trying to get their big break.

Nashville Musicians Services

11 Music Circle N.

P.O. Box 120399

Nashville, TN 37212

(615) 244-9514

www.nashvillemusicians.org

ACUFF-ROSE PUBLISHING

Country music legend Roy Acuff and musician songwriter Fred Rose started Acuff-Rose Publishing back in the mid-1950s. Its mission was to make sure that songwriters, many of whom had been getting ripped off by other publishing companies, got their fair share of the profits from the songs they wrote.

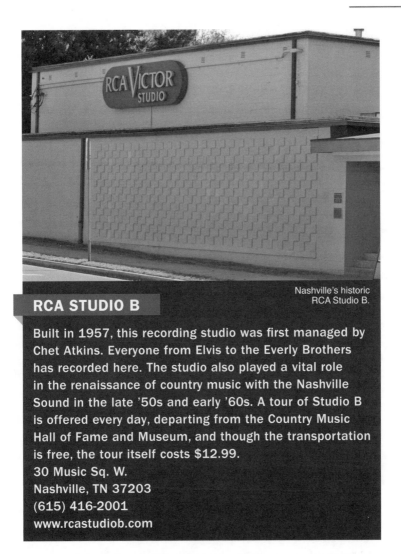

RCA STUDIO B

Nashville's historic RCA Studio B.

Built in 1957, this recording studio was first managed by Chet Atkins. Everyone from Elvis to the Everly Brothers has recorded here. The studio also played a vital role in the renaissance of country music with the Nashville Sound in the late '50s and early '60s. A tour of Studio B is offered every day, departing from the Country Music Hall of Fame and Museum, and though the transportation is free, the tour itself costs $12.99.
30 Music Sq. W.
Nashville, TN 37203
(615) 416-2001
www.rcastudiob.com

Music Publishing 101

I can't stress how important understanding the music publishing side of the business is. Years ago, I met a singer-songwriter and she said to me, "I really want to get a record deal with ASCAP." My jaw nearly dropped, and when I told her that ASCAP wasn't a record label, *her* jaw nearly dropped.

We all know that a lot of songs can be played using only three chords. So I want you to think of music publishing in the same way. We can all agree that there is always more to be learned, but if you grasp just the basics of music publishing, you will be a lot further along than your peers. There use to be a time years ago when songwriters would walk up and down Music Row knocking on doors and pitching their music to music publishing companies. The key words here are *years ago*. These days, that practice is a surefire way to get you nowhere. Having said that, songwriters still do it, which amazes me, but it screams to any music publisher that you just don't get it. Therefore, I met up with Mark Weiss at Ten Ten Music, a music publishing company along Music Row, and in the spirit of keeping it simple, asked him to spell out the nuts and bolts of music publishing.

Interview:
Mark Weiss, Director of Business Affairs, Ten Ten Music Group

Hometown: Kissimmee, FL

Liam Sullivan: What does a music publisher do?

Mark Weiss: A music publisher represents a songwriter and the rights for the songs created by that songwriter on his or her behalf. A publisher not only handles the administration, registration, and royalties of the writer's song but also arranges, co-writes, critiques, and helps to hone the writer's strengths, and tries to find the right fit for the works [or] songs for possible uses. So a music publisher handles the administrative as well as creative representation for a songwriter.

LS: What is the best approach as a songwriter to get a publishing deal? What's the process?

MW: Write great songs and get your songs heard. That is the best approach.

LS: Oh, okay, that was easy. Thank you for your time.

MW: [*Laughs*] In all seriousness, a songwriter should try to not only write by himself, but try and write with co-writers when possible. Do co-writers you know have a publishing deal? If so, how is it and can they recommend a good publisher? Talk with the folks at NSAI [National Songwriters Association International]. Play them your songs and tell them your songwriting dreams. Do the same with the writer relations representatives at the PROs, and ask them if they think you are ready for a publishing deal. If that's the case, ask if they can hook you up with some music publishers. Finally, continue to play out. The chances of your songs being heard not only by music fans, but also a music publisher, future co-writer, or a waitress who has a brother that works at a label here in Nashville are much greater when you play out. Word gets around and from that word of mouth your chances of getting a music publishing deal increase.

LS: Do music publishers go to open mic/writers' nights? If so and they hear a songwriter they like, will they go up to the songwriter after they are done playing and introduce themselves?

MW: Every segment of the music industry in Nashville goes to open mic songwriter nights. Where else can you see live raw talent? Sure, Facebook and YouTube have turned into a 24/7 plethora of opportunity for songwriters, but as a music publisher I want to see and hear someone live, see how they perform, and see how the audience reacts to their songs. The other thing to remember is that you could be the greatest songwriter in the world, but if you have a bad attitude and you are impossible to work with, I'd rather not even be associated with you. You're a professional and showing a respect for your craft and the audience you're playing for is paramount. So yes, music publishers definitely go to open mic/writers' nights and the great thing about this town is you never know who is going to be in the audience.

LS: Before entering into a relationship with a music publisher, does a songwriter need to have a manager?

MW: No. There is no need for a songwriter to have a manager in regards to his or her songs. The only time a songwriter would need a manager is if the songwriter was also an artist who needed someone to handle those duties.

LS: Sorry, I'm not sure I know what you mean. So when does a songwriter need to get a manager?

MW: Depending on the level of success that an artist has, they may need a personal manager or business manager, or someone to handle the bookings, publicity, finances, and other managerial stuff on behalf of the artist. A songwriter who only writes doesn't have these needs. You have to remember, there are plenty of very successful songwriters here in Nashville that no one has ever heard of. They are the songwriters who are behind the scenes, and they write songs that get picked by top country artists like Garth Brooks or Alan Jackson. On the flip side of that you have songwriters and performers here in Nashville that want to be the next Garth Brooks or Reba. As a songwriter, you have to figure out which side of that coin you want to be on. Do you want to write songs for the greats or do you want to be the one up there center stage. That's a decision only a songwriter can make for him or herself.

LS: Okay, so I'm playing out, I'm networking and honing my craft, but I'm still not getting any bites from a music publisher. How do I get permission and approval to send you my materials or songs?

MW: Generally, publishers will not accept cold calls. If they did, it would take up all of their time. Getting the attention of a music publisher can take time, but if you are getting positive feedback from everyone, continue what you're doing and look for opportunities to play for publishers. Again, talk with your PRO writer relations person about direction and opportunities. Their relationship with the writers and music publishers down on Music Row is an invaluable source to you as a songwriter.

LS: Okay, but let's say for example you see a songwriter at an open mic/writers' night and you like what you hear. What is the follow-up? What does the songwriter need to send you so that you have a better sense of who they are? A CD, website, Bio, lyric sheets, PRO affiliation, etc.?

MW: A publisher first and foremost wants to hear a great song, a song that makes them do back-flips! All that other stuff like bios and headshots are important, but it's all about the song. I don't care if it's on a CD, MP3, or played live at a gig. I just want to hear a great song. With that in mind, I'd like for a writer to have creativity, a passion for the craft, a good work ethic and self-discipline, and preferably, a means to play, sing, and record their songs. These are the things every music publisher is looking for. If I hear a great song, I'm not going to take a pass on that songwriter just because their headshot was taken in a weird color of sepia. As a publisher, all I need is a CD, an MP3, or a link with a handful of their best songs, the song information [writers/publishers], and the writer's contact info. Personally, I like a demo that allows me to hear every aspect of the song, instead of an a cappella version recorded on a boom box in the kitchen. Try to make it look and sound the best you can without going to extremes. Remember, you are trying to basically sell your songs, and if you aren't willing to invest the time and resources to make your songs the best they can be, then why should others invest their time in listening?

LS: If a music publisher hears a song at an open mic/writers' night that hasn't been recorded, will the music publisher pay to have that song recorded as a demo or work tape?

MW: They might pay as part of a single-song agreement. If a song was recorded as a demo that a publisher is interested in, the publisher might include reimbursement of the demo costs as part of the writer/publisher deal. However, most songwriter deals include language that has the publisher paying demo costs on behalf of the writer, up to a certain amount, which is usually $500 per song. That amount is then recoupable from future earnings that the song makes.

LS: In your opinion, what are some of the most common mistakes that songwriters make when they first get to Nashville?

MW: New songwriters often don't play out enough and still expect Music Row to come knocking down their door. It's about honing your skills. It's about learning and adapting. It's about playing out, and getting audience reaction to your songs. And of course, it's about networking.

LS: Can a music publisher help get a songwriter a record deal?

MW: Definitely. Publishers work hand in hand with the labels. Think about it this way. I'm a music publisher and I have a great songwriter, I pitch their songs to a label and the label thinks, "Wow, these are great songs" If the label ends up signing the writer to a record deal to cut their songs on a record, who do you think benefits besides the writer and the label? The music publisher. Why? Because the music publisher controls the rights to the writer's song. It's a great scenario for everyone involved.

LS: What is the difference between a music publisher and a publisher that just handles a songwriter's administration, aka admin., publisher?

MW: A music publisher controls the rights and collects royalties from licensees, record labels, film [and] TV, karaoke, game companies, etc. A music publisher also critiques songs, schedules co-writes, pitches the catalog of songs, and administers the writer's songs. The publisher could also have an exclusive deal in which they provide an advance to the songwriter. An administrator is generally only granted the right to administer a writer's songs for a limited amount of time, and for a fee. This fee can be a percentage, generally around 10 to 20 percent of the royalties, or it can be an hourly fee. If a writer is not earning a lot of money from a lot of sources, there is really no need to enter into an administrative publishing deal.

LS: If a songwriter gets a music publishing deal, what is the monetary percentage split between songwriter and music publisher once a song starts making some money?

MW: Generally fifty-fifty.

LS: How does a songwriter set up their own music publishing company? What are the costs for setting that up, and what are the advantages?

MW: Anyone can apply and affiliate with one of the PROs online as a music publisher and hit the ground running. With that in mind, anyone can cook, but does that mean everyone should open a restaurant? To be successful, you want a music publisher to represent you because they have the connections, they know what they are doing, and can make things happen for you as a writer. After all, that's what you are. A songwriter. Yes, it's good to control 100 percent of your own songs by having your own publishing company. My suggestion is to first focus on what you love and do best. Write songs.

LS: If a songwriter leaves one music publisher and goes with another, what happens to all those songs that the songwriter wrote for the first music publisher?

MW: Under an exclusive contract, you have assigned the rights to all songs written during the contractual term with the first publisher, which means they will remain with the first music publisher.

LS: But the songwriter still gets paid royalties if those songs are used by the first publisher, right?

MW: Yes.

LS: What is a "royalty"?

MW: A writer's royalty is income the songwriter receives as a payment for use of the songwriter's song or songs.

LS: When and why does a songwriter get paid by a PRO?

MW: A songwriter can expect to receive royalties from their PRO when their song is performed publicly—for example, if their song is performed or broadcasted on TV, radio, [the] Internet, etc. Generally, these royalties are processed and paid directly to the writer six to nine months after their domestic performances.

LS: So that payment doesn't go to the music publisher first? You mentioned earlier that a music publisher handles the royalties for a songwriter's song?

MW: Correct. Writers receive their performance royalties directly from the PRO they are affiliated with.

LS: What does it mean to license a song out? What's the process?

MW: Licensing a song is basically giving someone—the "licensee"— the right to reproduce, distribute, publicly perform, or create a derivative work of the songwriter's song. The licensing process begins with a request for use, followed by an agreement of terms and fees, and ends with proper payment to the songwriter and publisher.

LS: And where do those requests to use a songwriter's song come from?

MW: Basically, it can be from anyone. The requests can come from a major record label or from a girl in Oregon wanting to make and sell a CD of your song. It could be a request to use your song in a karaoke bar in Japan, or the background music in a major motion picture. The opportunities are limitless and a good publisher is the best way to exploit songs, create opportunities, and generate various revenue streams. However, in the end, they just need the songs!

> **66 For me, singing sad songs often has a way of healing a situation. It gets the hurt out in the open into the light, out of the darkness.99** —Reba McEntire

Top Music Publishing Terms Every Musician Should Know

Once you've gotten to the point where you're working with a music publisher before any of your songs are released for usage, you as the songwriter have rights. These rights protect you, and they make sure that you are getting paid for your songs. As we all know, there are various distribution platforms out there these days where a song can land up—for example a CD, iTunes, a TV commercial, a movie soundtrack, or on the Internet. When that happens, having an understanding of the terms used in those types of different agreements is in your best interest. Therefore, here is a breakdown of some of the most commonly used terms when dealing with a music publisher.

Publishing Deal

You will hear this term a lot in Nashville and down on Music Row. If a music publisher really likes your music, you could potentially enter into what's called a publishing deal. Here's how it works: A music publisher pays you an advance. It's not free money; it's a loan. Your job is to deliver a great song or songs. The publisher will then pitch that great song. If it turns out that the great song you wrote is picked up by some big-time artist, the money earned will basically act as payback for the money that the publisher lent you in the first place. Once that loan or advance is paid back in full, that's when you, the songwriter, start to make money.

Mechanical Rights or Mechanical Royalties

This is money you receive from the commercial use of your song released for sale, via such avenues as CD sales, ringtones, streams, and downloads from iTunes.

Statutory Mechanical Royalty Rate

This is the royalty amount for a song use on a CD, iTunes, etc. Currently, that rate is 9.1 cents per song.

Synchronization Rights, or "Sync Rights"

"Sync rights" refer to the use of your song in connection with visual elements. The publisher will negotiate these rights on your behalf, and the amount can vary depending on the length and use of your song in a film, television program, webisode, video, or other form of audio/visual means.

Performance Rights

These rights cover all public performances of your song, including live performances, television broadcast, and radio use. All are paid directly from the PROs. Both the writer and the publisher are each paid directly from the PRO they belong to. But remember, as a songwriter you can affiliate with only one PRO at a time.

Co-publishing Deal

When you sign a co-publishing deal, you're entering into a legal agreement of percentages with a publisher. Example: You have a song. Publisher wants song. You and publisher work out a co-publishing deal, which is usually a fifty-fifty split on the money made from the song. This is generally an option only (a) after proven prior success from the songwriter or (b) if the songwriter is signed to a record deal.

Master

Rights surrounding the actual recording of a song or songs, most often controlled by the record label.

All In

All-in rights include the publishing "sync" side, and the label "master" side.

Advance

Also referred to as a "draw," the advance is a recoupable "paycheck" paid in advance by a music publisher to a writer to write songs.

Transfer of Assignment

This term describes the handing-over of copyright ownership between a publisher and a songwriter.

Most-Favored Nation Basis

No other party will get better terms or paid more for the same use. For example: If your song is one of six songs used in the TV show *Glee*, and it is licensed on a most-favored nation basis, then that means you are guaranteed to receive no less than what the other five songs will receive in terms of payment and conditions.

Exclusive Agreement

This is an agreement between the songwriter and publisher that the songwriter writes for the publisher exclusively, generally up to twelve songs a year. Therefore, everything the songwriter writes during the time of the agreement period, is controlled by the music publisher.

Single-Song Agreement

Unlike an exclusive agreement, a single-song agreement transfers the rights for a specific song, to be represented by the publisher for a certain period of time.

Perpetuity

Simply put it means "forever." If you enter into a deal with your publisher and the publisher wants perpetuity, it means they want to have ownership of that song forever.

Life of Copyright

This term refers to the life of the song you have copyrighted with a publisher. These days, it is the length of time that you live plus seventy years before the copyright becomes public domain.

Public Domain

When a copyright expires, the song becomes public domain, meaning anyone can use it for free.

Grace Quebe at the Station Inn, Nashville.

MUSIC PUBLISHING RESOURCE

There is a good resource for beginners and professionals who want to contact music publishers in Nashville and around the country. The website below offers up information on which companies allow material submissions and their specific requirements for doing so. www.songwritersource.com

Song and Music Publishers in Nashville

Air Deluxe Music Group

23 Music Sq. E.

Nashville, TN 37203

(615) 726-1204

www.airdeluxemusic.com

Big Loud Shirt

1111 16th Ave. S.

Nashville, TN 37212

(615) 329-1929

www.bigloudshirt.com

Bluewater Music

1222 16th Ave. S.

Nashville, TN 37212

(615) 327-0808

www.bluewatermusic.com

BUG Music

33 Music Sq. W.

Nashville, TN 37203

(615) 313-7676

www.bugmusic.com

Carnival Music

24 Music Sq. W.

Nashville, TN 37203

(615) 259-0841

www.carnivalmusic.com

Courtyard Music

118 Sixth Ave. S.

Nashville, TN 37203

(615) 533-7756

www.courtyardmusicgroup.com

Curb Music Publishing

48 Music Sq. E.

Nashville, TN 37203

(615) 321-5080

www.curb.com

Full Circle

1225 17th Ave. S.

Nashville, TN 37212

(615) 321-8686

www.fullcirclemusicpublishing.com

Peermusic

702 18th Ave. S.

Nashville, TN 37203

(615) 329-0603

www.peermusic.com

Roots Three Music

1227 16th Ave. S.

Nashville, TN 37212

(615) 327-2645

www.rootsthree.com

> In 1950, a Grand Ole Opry announcer named David Cobb coined the phrase "Music City USA" for the first time, referring to Nashville being a major music hub in the country.

Music Education

Belmont University

One of the best things about Belmont University is that it is located at the base of Music Row. Students interested in pursuing a career in the music business will find that there is a natural symmetry between Belmont and Music Row. Most if not all music businesses along Music Row offer internships. Depending on what field you want to study, Belmont offers a wide range of courses from music publishing to music producing.

1900 Belmont Blvd.

Nashville, TN 37212

Main: (615) 460-6000

Undergraduate admissions: (615) 460-6785

www.belmont.edu

Bluegrass banjos.

Mike Curb College of Entertainment and Music Business

Mike Curb College is affiliated with Belmont.

34 Music Sq. E.

Nashville, TN 37212

(615) 460-6000

www.belmont.edu

MTSU Middle Tennessee State University

Located about forty minutes from downtown Nashville in
Murfreesboro, Tennessee, MTSU has one of the best music programs
around. MTSU's School of Music offers courses covering everything
from general music education, voice performance, music theory,
and composition to instrumental performance.

1301 E. Main St.

Murfreesboro, TN 37132

Main: (615) 898-2300

Undergraduate admissions: (615) 898-2111

www.mtsu.edu

SAE (Music Education Career)

7 Music Circle N.

Nashville, TN 37203

(615) 244-5848

www.nashville.sae.edu

Interview:
Dr. Don Cusic, Professor of Music Business, Belmont University

Liam Sullivan: How did you find your way to Nashville?

Don Cusic: Well, I'm originally from Maryland and had wanted to come to Nashville ever since I was a kid. After I graduated from the University of Maryland, I built a bed in the back of my VW van and moved to Tennessee. I lived in that van for the first five months when I first got here, and I started knocking away at trying to get into the music scene. If you bang your head against the wall long enough it will crack—whether it's your head or the wall, that's the question. [*Laughs*]

LS: So how did you get into the music scene here in Nashville?

DC: I had played in country bands but I came here to Nashville to be a songwriter. I could hold my own when it came to playing guitar but when you get here it is a whole other level. It's major league here, and there are guitarists that will just blow you out of the water.

I had some success writing some songs and did some recordings but because I had a degree in journalism I wanted to go in that direction.

LS: What were some of the things you did to survive when you first got to Nashville?

DC: When I got to Nashville I started doing some writing for a new music magazine that had just started up. I was then introduced to a guy who was looking for someone who could conduct interviews with the top people in country music. He said, "If you can help me out with that, I can buy you a hamburger every now and again." So that worked for me. [*Laughs*] That led to getting a job at CMA [Country Music Association], writing for them. So I had gone from living in my car to getting a job and finally getting a little place of my own.

LS: Were you still playing music?

DC: No, I quit. But when it comes to singer-songwriters who want to come to Nashville, there's an old saying that goes, "He who sings will always find a song." Songwriters tend to be introverted, but in this town you have to meet people, and where do you meet people is mostly in churches and bars or both. That's why the open mic/writers' nights here in Nashville are so important, because you have to get outside of yourself and introduce yourself. Sometimes that's a hard thing for a songwriter, but you can't wait for the music business to come and worship at your doorstep. Someone once said about coming to Nashville, "You might not believe in God, but you better hope that he believes in you."

LS: What advice would you give a singer-songwriter who's looking for a job in the music business?

DC: The problem with getting a job in the music business for a songwriter is that it takes your mind away from songwriting. Kris

Kristofferson wouldn't do it. He bartended, he cleaned recording studios to get by. [If you're] a songwriter, you want a job that takes your body but not your mind, because you want your mind for writing songs. And if you work in an office, it takes your mind.

LS: What kinds of things did you learn from getting out there and meeting other people at an open mic writers' night, for example?

DC: Well, there are two parts to songwriting: There's the art and the craft. People who come to Nashville just want to learn the art, but there is a craft to writing songs. That's what you learn from getting out and being around professional songwriters at writers' nights. People come to Belmont University all the time and say, "I just want to write for myself." Amateurs write for themselves; professionals write for an audience. If you want to go off and write songs for yourself, then fine, but we're here to make money. This is a business, and songwriters often forget that part.

LS: What do you think it takes for a songwriter to become successful?

DC: I learned this by playing music myself: You get to a point or level where you realize that you're only going to go so far. People who become successful have drive and talent, so even if you have the basic skills, that just might not be enough. So eventually, here in Nashville, songwriters weed themselves out. The other thing is that you have to give up a lot to become a top performer, and there is very little balance. The first thing that you give up is family and a home. A lot of people wouldn't mind being a star if it wasn't so much trouble. To be successful it takes 110 percent, and people realize that once they get some success. People think it's all about the hour up on stage in the lights. It takes the other twenty-three hours of hard, hard work to get up there.

LS: You mentioned the craft of songwriting. Can you elaborate on that.

DC: You have to play all the time. Look at Willie Nelson: He's jamming all the time, on and off stage, on the tour bus, and he's playing his own songs as well as cover songs. The guy is always playing. A lot of songwriters say that they don't want to play cover songs, but that's how you learn. Most songwriters want to pick up their guitars and start venting about what's on their mind, but that doesn't help expand your craft. If you just want to play the songs you've written, you're going to be limited, because what you want is to expand your musical horizon, and the best way to do that is to play with others and sit around and jam.

LS: That's a great point. How does that relate to networking?

DC: This is a co-writing town. You can write a song either by yourself or with someone else and get a cut [song] picked up by a major artist and or a music publishing company, and that's a great revenue stream.

LS: How does that work, exactly?

DC: What most music publishers do is they depend on their existing songwriters on staff to bring in new songwriters. So if you go to a writers' night and strike up a conversation and try and start co-writing with another songwriter, that's a great approach. If something you've written catches their ear, then they'll tell their music publisher. The other benefit to co-writing is that it doubles your exposure, because every songwriter you meet has other songwriter friends that you could possible write with. When you meet one person, you're never meeting just one person; you're meeting a whole new group of people. Everyone has friends and contacts, so in this process you are building your own networking base. Again, the key thing is, you have to get out there and play and introduce yourself. I'm reminded of a line from a Robert Frost poem that says, "Way leads to way," and that's how it goes in this town: You meet one person and it takes off from there.

LS: If I'm not a student here at Belmont, what are some of the resources I can tap into?

DC: We have students here who have to put together projects where they find an act, promote a band. We also have showcases throughout the year that feature urban, pop, country, Christian, and rock, and they are posted on the Belmont website.

HEADSHOTS

Along with having a CD, lyric sheets, and a website, you will no doubt at some point have to look into the camera and say, "Cheese." A headshot is another one of those basic necessities for all songwriters.

Headshots Nashville
2108 19th Ave. S.
Nashville, TN 37212
(615) 460-7818
www.headshotsnashville.com

66 **You can't stay the same. If you're a musician and a singer, you have to change. That's the way it works.** 99 —Van Morrison

Music Row, Nashville.

Recording Studios

Heading into the studio is one of those things that musicians love most. However, the reasons for wanting to record can vary. Some songwriters and bands may want to record an entire album or just do a demo for a music publisher to listen to. No two studios are alike, so it's not a bad idea to take a look around before you commit, because the one thing that musicians don't like about heading into the studio is the cost.

Alex the Great Recording

708 Fessey Park Rd.

Nashville, TN 37204

(615) 385-5467

www.alexthegreat.com

Catch This Music

1008 17th Ave. S.

Nashville, TN 37212

(615) 340-9000

www.catchthismusic.com

Direct Image Recording Studio

1700 Hayes St.

Nashville, TN 37203

(615) 321-8532

www.directimagestudio.com

Fun House

802 18th Ave. S.

Nashville, TN 37212

(615) 242-7949

www.funhousestudios.com

Germantown Recording Studio

1209 4th Ave. N.

Nashville, TN 37208

(615) 244-8019

www.towereg.com

Hilltop Recording Studio

902 Due West Ave.

Nashville, TN 37115

(615) 865-5272

www.hilltopstudio.com

OMNI sound Recording Studio

1806 Division St.

Nashville, TN 37204

(615) 482-1511

www.omnisoundstudios.com

Sweetbriar Recording Studio

2036 Priest Rd.

Nashville, TN 37204

(615) 210-2120

www.sweetbriarrecording.com

The Toy Box Studio

2407 Brasher Ave

Nashville, TN 37206

(615) 262-1374

www.thetoyboxstudio.com

Verge Recordings

2409 21st Ave.

Nashville, TN 37212

(615) 320-5576

www.vergenashville.com

Waterworks Recording Studio

P.O. Box 120333

Nashville, TN 37212

(615) 262-0405

www.waterworksentertainment.com

Welcome to 1979 Studio

1110 48th Ave. N.

Nashville, TN 37209

(615) 476-6272

www.welcometo1979.com

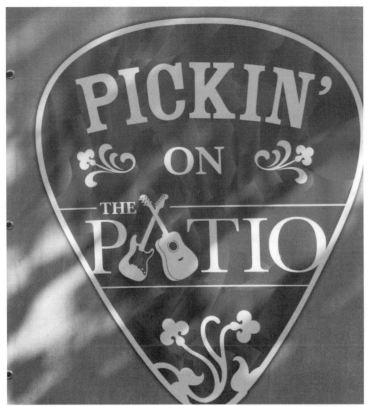

Pickin' and grinning. Music Row, Nashville.

Talent Agencies

APA (Agency for the Performing Arts)

3010 Poston Ave.

Nashville, TN 37203

(615) 297-0100

www.apa-agency.com

Buddy Lee Attractions

38 Music Sq. E., Ste. 300

Nashville, TN 37203

(615) 244-4336

www.buddyleeattractions.com

CAA Creative Artists Agency

3310 West End Ave., 5th Fl.

Nashville, TN 37203

(615) 383-8787

www.caatouring.com

William Morris Endeavor Entertainment

1600 Division St., Ste. 300

Nashville, TN 37203

(615) 963-3364

www.wmeentertainment.com

Record Labels in Nashville

Arista Nashville

1400 18th Ave. S.

Nashville, TN 37212

(615) 301-4300

www.aristanashville.com

Capitol Records Nashville

3322 West End Ave.

Nashville, TN 37203

(615) 269-2000

www.capitolnashville.com

Carnival Recording Company

24 Music Sq. W.

Nashville, TN 37203

(615) 259-0841

www.carnivalrecording.com

Castle Records

30 Music Sq. W.

Nashville, TN 37203

(615) 401-7111

www.castlerecords.com

Compass Records

916 19th Ave. S.

Nashville, TN 37212

(615) 320-7672

www.compassrecords.com

Curb Records

48 Music Sq. E.

Nashville, TN 37203

(615) 321-5080

www.curb.com

Lost Highway Records

401 Commerce St., Ste. 1100

Nashville, TN 37219

(615) 524-7848

www.losthighwayrecords.com

MCA Nashville

401 Commerce St., Ste. 1100

Nashville, TN 37219

(615) 524-7500

www.umgnashville.com

Mercury Records

401 Commerce St., Ste. 1100

Nashville, TN 37219

(615) 524-7500

www.umgnashville.com

RCA Nashville

1400 18th Ave. S.

Nashville, TN 37212

www.rcanashville.com

Warner Brothers Records

20 Music Sq. E.

Nashville, TN 37203

(615) 748-8000

www.wbrnashville.com

BLUEGRASS BREAKDOWN

The Bluegrass Breakdown was the name of the tour bus used by the Father of Bluegrass, Bill Monroe, during the 1970s. Ferlin Husky originally owned the vehicle; he sold it to the Queen of Country Music, Kitty Wells, and she eventually sold it to Bill Monroe, who also wrote an instrumental piece by the same name. *Bluegrass Breakdown* is also a radio program that airs every Saturday night on Nashville's own 90.3 FM WPLN

Hulda Quebe playing with soul.

CD/DVD Duplication

Disc Makers

1305 16th Ave. S., 1st Fl.

Nashville, TN 37212

(615) 321-6275

www.discmakers.com

Ear Mark Digital

1019 16th Ave. S.

Nashville, TN 37212

(615) 329-1070

www.earmarkdigital.com

We Make Tapes and Discs

118 16th Ave. S., Ste. 1

Nashville, TN 37203

(888) 271-3472

www.wemaketapes.com

The Station Inn, Nashville.

Music Instrument Stores

Corner Music

Whether helping customers purchase home recording equipment, used instruments, or some new gear, Corner Music prides itself on working with individuals to find the right fit. They also have a great selection of boutique amps and vintage guitars.

2705 12th Ave. S.

Nashville, TN 37204

(615) 297-9559

www.cornermusic.com

Forks Drum Closet

Drums and more drums. There are also in-store postings if you're looking for a drummer for your band. If you're a drummer looking to improve your chops, Forks offers drum lessons at affordable prices with some of the best drummers in the world. Example? Chester Thompson, who has played with Frank Zappa, Weather Report, and Genesis, to name a few.

2701 12th Ave. S.

Nashville, TN 37204

(615) 383-8343

www.forksdrumcloset.com

Cotton Music

New/used/vintage guitar shop featuring some of the best brand names out there—Martin, Santa Cruz, Godin—and the all the accessories that go along with them, and all under one roof.

1815 21st Ave. S.

Nashville, TN 37212

(615) 383-8947

www.cottenmusic.com

Other good places to find instruments include:

Fanny's House of Music

1101 Holly St.

Nashville, TN 37206

(615) 750-5746

www.fannyshouseofmusic.com

GEAR REPAIR

These guys can virtually take any guitar in any kind of horrible condition and make it like new. So if your pick guard fell off your guitar or you decided to do your best Pete Townshend impression at the end of your gig, pick up the pieces and bring it to Glaser.

Glaser Instruments
434 E. Iris Dr.
Nashville, TN 37204
(615) 298-1139
www.glaserinstruments.com

Gruhn Guitars

400 Broadway

Nashville, TN 37203

(615) 256-2033

www.gruhn.com

Guitar Center

721 Thompson Lane

Nashville, TN 37204

(615) 297-7770

www.guitarcenter.com

Nashville Used Music

4876 Nolensville Rd.

Nashville, TN 37211

(615) 832-7450

www.nashvilleusedandnewmusic.com

Sam Ash

1647 Gallatin Pike

Madison, TN 37115

(615) 860-7475

www.samashmusic.com

World Music

7069 Hwy. 70 S.

Nashville, TN 37221

(615) 425-0256

There's no website so swing on by.

Gear Rental and Rehearsal Space

SIR

1101 Cherry Ave.

Nashville, TN 37203

(615) 255-4500

www.sir-usa.com

Soundcheck

750 Cowan St.

Nashville, TN 37207

(615) 726-1165

www.soundchecknashville.com

Record Stores

Ernest Tubb Record Shop,
lower Broadway, Nashville.

Ernest Tubb Record Shop

From old-time country to bluegrass to Texas swing, Ernest Tubb
Record Shop is a great place to check out after your tour of the
Country Music Hall of Fame and Museum and a place where you
can begin to build your own country music catalogue.

417 Broadway

Nashville, TN 37203

(615) 255-7503

www.etrecordshop.com

CD Warehouse

2143 Gallatin Pike N.

Madison, TN 37115

(615) 851-1835

www.cdwarehouseonline.com

FYE

2400 West End Ave.

Nashville, TN 37203

(615) 321-8582

www.fye.com

The Great Escape

5400 Charlotte Ave.

Nashville, TN 37209

(615) 327-0646

www.thegreatescapeonline.com

Grimey's

1604 Eighth Ave. S.

Nashville, TN 37203

(615) 254-4801

www.grimeys.com

The Groove

1103 Calvin Ave.

Nashville, TN 37206

(615) 227-5760

www.thegroovenashville.com

Lawrence Records

409 Broadway

Nashville, TN 37203

(615) 256-9240

www.lawrencerecordshop.com

McKay Used Books & CDs

5708 Charlotte Pike

Nashville, TN 37209

(615) 353-2595

www.mckaybooks.com

Phonoluxe

2609 Nolensville Pike

Nashville, TN 37211

(615) 259-3500

No website, so swing on by.

Third Man Records

623 Seventh Ave. S.

Nashville, TN 37203

(615) 891-4393

www.thirdmanrecords.com

In the 1950s, a variation of the Hawaiian steel guitar, "pedal steel," made its way into country music and western swing. The first hit song featuring the pedal steel sound was a song called "Slowly" by Web Pierce.

ASCAP, Music
Row, Nashville.

Interview:
Ralph Murphy, Vice President, International and Domestic Membership, ASCAP

I met up with Ralph at the Sunset Grill in Hillsboro Village for lunch and to talk about music and get his views on what a songwriter needs these days to make it in the music business.

Ralph credits Little Jimmy Dickens for getting him into music. Little Jimmy Dickens is a country singer and legend who has been a Grand Ole Opry member for sixty years and hosts the Opry to this day. As Ralph describes it, "I started playing a Hawaiian steel guitar by the age of eleven and I bought a piece of sheet music by Dickens with a picture of Little Jimmy on it called 'Sleeping at the Foot of the Bed.' Years later I finally met Little Jimmy backstage at the Grand Ole Opry, and I told him that story."

Liam Sullivan: So when you heard the Beatles and moved to Liverpool, did you want to become a rock star?

Ralph Murphy: No, I really just wanted to write songs. I understood the power of song from an early age when my mother taught me a song called "The Mountains of Mourne" by the Irish songwriter Percy French. [*Ralph begins to sing a verse from the song*] "Oh, Mary, this London's a wonderful sight, with people all working by day and by night. Sure, they don't sow potatoes, nor barley, nor wheat, But there's gangs of them digging for gold in the street." There are some really great verses. It's a long song, and when I first sang it in public it struck me that everyone was applauding the song, not me, and then it occurred to me, wouldn't it be cool to be the provider of songs that everyone wanted to sing? And that's why I started out writing.

LS: Can you explain that further?

RM: Well, most songwriters start out writing for cathartic reasons, to get stuff out of their system. There are three things that songwriters feel like they have a mandate to do when they discover the gift of songwriting and they are to whine, preach, and vent. Because you want to tell the world about "you," but the world doesn't care about you. That's a major problem for all songwriters.

LS: What do you mean?

RM: The biggest problem songwriters have [is] themselves, because they want to tell the world about them. The job, or the hurdle, for the professional songwriter is to get themselves out of the way and to write songs about you and give the listener "them" as you, the songwriter, see them. For me, I wanted to write songs that everybody gravitated toward, and so I needed to learn the craft and structure and discover who I was and I how I could get past me or get "over" me.

LS: So you have to find that common ground between you the songwriter and the listener.

RS: Yes, but then you have to invite them in. You have to find something that resonates with them. At the same time, you have to make the singer look good to them.

LS: What do you mean?

RM: Well, let's take women, for example. Women hear differently than men speak. When a relationship ends for a woman, 100 percent of the time it's the man's fault. So if a guy gets up on stage and sings, "Since you left me," the women in the audience will say to themselves, "Jerk, he must have done something wrong to her." So instead of feeling bad for that guy singing his heart out onstage, women think, "Creep." So what the guy should sing is, "Since she left him," and then tell the story about it. Remember, it's not about you. Get *you* out of the way.

LS: That's an interesting point.

RM: Yeah, when people come out to see you play live, there is a different dynamic. Let's take the Bluebird café, for example: The food is great, they have a great wine list, and the beer is really cold, so you have all that and then there is someone singing their heart out. At the end of the gig, when someone comes up to you and says, "I love your music," they don't mean that. What they really mean is that they love your personality, the venue, the food, the vibe—way down on the list is the song. When it comes to radio, all of that vibe stuff is taken away.

LS: Can you explain that further?

RM: Radio, that's where the money is. On radio the song is number one. The person listening doesn't have a glass of wine in front of them or all of those other distractions. Suddenly it's just a song talking to them about them. People who listen to radio are monumentally distracted; they're driving around picking up the kids. They don't have time to waste while you tinker and wander through two or three verses coming to a conclusion. They'll allow you forty-five seconds from the start of your vocal. That's all they allow you, and if you can't hook them, then they exclude you.

That's who you're dealing with; you are dealing with people who are predisposed to hate you. That's who you're writing for. [*We both laugh*]

LS: Wow, okay, well, don't sugarcoat it. What advice would you give a songwriter who wants to develop a persona?

RM: Keep the persona consistent. In today's country music, singer-songwriters do not change persona from song to song. For example, you'll never hear Kenny Chesney sing a song about children or having children—that's not who he is. Be who you are. If you're writing by yourself, you better define what you're all about. That, and you have to network and get to know and watch what other people are doing. You have to get out and meet other songwriters. Nashville is a hanging town, and in the end, you are the sum of the people you know.

LS: In your opinion, what would be the best approach for someone who is thinking of moving to Nashville to get involved and to establish themselves here as a songwriter?

RM: Do your research about Nashville before you leave your hometown. It helps to know the history of the place you're moving to. When you get here, rent a place on a short-term basis and figure out what neighborhood best fits your lifestyle; that could be East Nashville or down here near Music Row. The other thing is, when you get here, leave your guitar at home. Go out to a writers' night and just sit and watch. Go to the Listening Room or go down to Tootsies or the Bluebird Cafe and go to all the six o'clock shows. That's where your peer group is going to be hanging out. All the cats playing at 9:00 P.M. at a writers' night are the big dogs, and they're not your peer group. Your peer group will be the people who arrived on the same day you did. Again, you need to network and get a sense of all the venues before you play them.

LS: How would you go about networking if you were new to town?

RM: I would go to all the open mic/writers' nights, and if I saw someone whose music I really liked, I would introduce myself. If you compliment a songwriter, you'll have a friend for life.

LS: So lie?

RM: [*Laughs*] No, if you hear a song that a writer sings that resonates with you and is not radically offensive at an open mic night, go up and introduce yourself. Say, "Hey, I really liked that song about the dog or whatever. I'm new to town; maybe we could get to together and write?" Keep it friendly and exchange e-mail addresses or give them one of your CDs. But whatever you do, don't gherm.

LS: *Gherm*? What does that mean?

RM: To gherm means being relentlessly pushy or really in someone's face to the point that out of self-defense that person has to be rude and tell the ghermer to go away.

LS: Now you tell me!

RM: [*Laughs*]

LS: As a musician, what was the first big hit you had when you lived in London?

RM: "Call My Name" in 1966.

LS: Who recorded it?

RM: James Royal. We sold a million copies in Germany, Belgium, and France. I still get royalty checks from that song to this day.

LS: What did you do after you left London?

RM: I became a record producer and started doing work for CBS and Decca Records. Then I produced the band April Wine's first two albums that went platinum.

LS: When did you join ASCAP?

RM: By the time I joined ASCAP, I had done pretty much everything that I wanted to do in the music business. I had produced lots of records, had number one songs in all genres, and worked in theater, TV, and film. So I took the job at ASCAP because I felt that I could do a lot more [by] being on the inside and supporting other up-and-coming songwriters.

LS: What's the best advice for a songwriter who's trying to write a hit song?

RM: Well, you can't stop a great song in this town; eventually it will be heard and word will get around. You have to keep in mind who you're writing for. In the country music Nashville market, it's women twenty-five to forty-eight years old who are listening at 7:00 A.M. That's your audience. So you can never be a loser or over thirty years old in a song. Use a lot of pronouns and always make the artist who might sing your song one day look good. If you don't have a personality, rent one. [*Laughs*] You want to make people want to hang around you. Remember, you're never a loser and you're never over thirty in a song . . . *ever.*

"Pretty Woman," Music Row, Nashville.

Music Festivals

Bonnaroo Music Festival

What do you call an outdoor concert where 80,000 music enthusiasts prance around in the dirt, in ninety-degree heat, on seven hundred acres of open land in Manchester, Tennessee? The answer is Bonnaroo, and it is probably the closest thing to this side of the Summer of Love and Woodstock that you'll ever experience. Held each June, this festival features one main stage, where big acts such as the Police, Dave Matthews Band, and Bruce Springsteen have performed. There are also a series of smaller stages spread out over the festival grounds, which, depending on the vantage point, can either look like Dante's Inferno or a small city where the residents have gone happily mad. On these smaller stages, there's a wide array of music acts ranging from hip-hop to blues, country, and alternative. If the music gets to you and you need a break, there's a cinema, an arcade, and a comedy club. Showers are available for a fee during daylight hours, and Bonnaroo has got more portable bathroom units than Flushing Meadows.

With that said, Bonnaroo is extremely well organized and unites people from all walks of life for four days of music, food, and sleeping under the stars. So bring your lighter for the rock ballads, water for hydration, and all the stamina you can muster. Believe me, you're going to need it.

For more information about the festival:

www.bonnaroo.com

Tin Pan South

It has been suggested in this book that a visit during the Tin Pan South music festival would be a good way to get a flavor of Nashville before you move here. Held each spring, Tin Pan South plays host to some of the best songwriters and musicians around. Over the course of five days, every live music venue in town is booked, with hundreds of performances held each night. It is a great event at which to see and hear what other singer-songwriters are up to, and you can begin to network and get a sense of the city at the same time. It's practically a musician's paradise!

For more information about the festival:

www.tinpansouth.com

Both jazz and bluegrass are homegrown. Both genres are unique and indigenous to America's musical landscape.

CMA Music Festival

Held in June each year, the CMA Music Festival causes Nashville's population to majorly spike. Tens of thousands of country music fans from around the world and beyond show up to see country music's biggest stars perform at LP Field, which otherwise is Nashville's main sports stadium, located right across the river from downtown Nashville. You can line up and get autographs and pictures taken with your favorite country artists. There are exhibits and a block party along with several outdoor concerts held downtown along the river during the entire week.

For more information about the festival:

www.cmaworld.com

Like no other place in the world.
Lower Broadway, Nashville.

Bluegrass Fan Fest

Sponsored by the International Bluegrass Music Association and held each September, this festival offers bluegrass fans the chance to not only see their favorite artists perform but to meet them as well. This festival is very laid-back and features some of the best guitar, mandolin, and banjo players in bluegrass today.

For more information about the festival:

www.bluegrassfanfest.org

Next Big Nashville

In the spirit of SXSW (South by Southwest), Next Big Nashville is a five-day event held in the fall each year, and features a wide range of music genres highlighting mostly Nashville bands and songwriters. They have also swung the doors open in recent years, and now feature big name acts from around the country, attracting more attendees while reinforcing the claim that Nashville is an all-inclusive music town.

For more information about the festival:

www.nbnsoundland.com

Rites of Spring Music Festival

Held each spring—imagine that!—on the Vanderbilt University campus, this festival attracts well-known national acts along with whatever bands are being played on the local university radio station at 2:00 A.M. Tickets are reasonably priced, the festival is outdoors, and since Vanderbilt is so close to downtown and all points east, west, north, and south, you can leave the car at home and take a cab, avoiding the parking nightmare altogether.

For more information about the festival:

www.vanderbilt.edu/ros

Americana Music Festival and Conference

This is another festival that you might want to consider if you're thinking of taking a trip to Nashville to get a better sense of the lay of the land. Apart from live music, there are also panels held during the day with music industry professionals that cover every topic of the music business. So the event is both entertaining and educational. The festival is held each September, which is a great time to visit Nashville: The temperatures are below the bake level but still warm enough that you can enjoy a cool sweet tea.

For more information about the festival and conference:

www.americanamusic.org

Uncle Dave Macon Days

Also known as the "Dixie Dewdrop," Uncle Dave Macon was an early-twentieth-century phenomenon. He cut his teeth during the early years of vaudeville and was a vital part of the very first barn dances, which would eventually spawn the *Grand Ole Opry*, which aired on WSM radio back in 1925. Uncle Dave's unique banjo playing made him a standout. One of his onstage tricks was to toss his banjo in the air and catch it without missing a beat. Uncle Dave Macon Days is a festival held each July in memory of him in Murfreesboro, Tennessee, which is about a forty-minute drive from Nashville. Macon died in Murfreesboro in 1952. The festival features banjo, dulcimer, guitar, and dancing contests, as well as a parade of horse-drawn carriages and a wide array of food vendors. A throwback to simpler times? Perhaps, but this festival is a true slice of Americana.

For more information about the festival:

www.uncledavemacondays.com

NASHVILLE SMACK-DAB

It can be argued that geographically Nashville is at the very epicenter of some of the most important music genres to have evolved in the United States. To the east in the foothills of Appalachia is where old-time music and country found its footing. To the west, in Memphis, the blues, rock and roll, rockabilly, and soul flourished, with Stax Records and Sun Studio leading the charge. To the north, Kentucky bluegrass is king, and to the south, New Orleans is famous for its jazz. Sitting smack-dab in the middle of all that is Nashville.

Radio Programs for Musicians

WPLN 90.3 FM

American Routes, Saturdays, 10:00 P.M.

Bluegrass Breakdown, Saturdays, 9:00 P.M.

Live at the Bluebird Cafe, Saturdays, 7:00 P.M.

WSM 650 AM

Bluegrass Underground, one Saturday a month (see "Road Trips")

Grand Ole Opry Live, Fridays and Saturdays, 7:00 P.M.

Live at the Station Inn, second Thursday each month, 3:00 P.M.–7:00 P.M.

WRLT FM 100, "Lightning 100"

Live simulcast from music venue 3rd and Lindsley, Sundays, 8:00 P.M.

THE BILLY BLOCK SHOW

Held at the Rutledge every Tuesday night, this show, broadcast on WKDF 103.3 FM, features some of Nashville's best songwriters and bands. The Rutledge is a great venue, and the show is a great way to network and spend a Tuesday evening.
For more information go to:
www.billyblock.com
www.therutledgelmv.com

Radio Stations

Country and Bluegrass Music Radio Stations

WQSV 790 AM

WSM 650 AM

WKDF 103.3 FM

WSIX 97.9 FM

Rock Stations

WBUZ 102.9 FM

WNRQ 105.9 FM

College Radio Stations

WFSK 88.1 FM, Fisk University

WMTS 88.3 FM, Middle Tennessee State University

WRVU 91.1 FM, Vanderbilt University

Satellite Country Radio

Sirius XM Country Music Channels

Bluegrass Junction

The Highway

Outlaw Country

Prime Country

The Roadhouse

Great American Country,
Music Row, Nashville.

Country Music TV Stations

CMT (Country Music Television)

Back when MTV broke new ground by introducing an all-music-video format, the one obvious omission within the lineup was country music videos. So the good folks at CMT decided to get in on the act. Today CMT still plays music videos and airs various weekly shows, on which some of the biggest names in country music are interviewed. The good thing about CMT is that you don't need to be in Nashville to watch it. It's everywhere. Check local listings.

GAC (Great American Country)

Yet another channel dedicated to playing country music videos, GAC also airs the big country awards show American Country Awards each year. So the way I see it, there really isn't any reason not to watch.

> In 1955, the first recording studio was built by Owen Bradley down on Music Row. A statue of him playing piano sits at the top of Music Row.

THE MARTY STUART SHOW

This country variety show airs on Saturday nights at 8:00 P.M. ET. The lineup of artists performing live on the show is breathtaking, with names such as Willie Nelson, the Carolina Chocolate Drops, and Loretta Lynn guesting. This is the kind of show that leaves you wanting more. *The Marty Stuart Show* airs on RFD-TV, and it can be found on channel 136 through Comcast cable in Nashville.

For more information about *The Marty Stuart Show* and where you can get RFD-TV in your neck of the woods, go to:

The Marty Stuart Show
Tickets
3201 Dickerson Pike
Nashville, TN 37207
(615) 227-9292
www.rfdtv.com

Music Magazines

MusicRow

This is a great resource for those who want to keep up on the latest news regarding the music industry down on Music Row. The magazine has record reviews and a list of the biggest songs making their way up the charts. There are also interviews with well-known artists and smaller features highlighting new up-and-coming songwriters in the music industry.

1231 17th Ave. S.
Nashville, TN 37212
(615) 349-2171
www.musicrow.com

Nashville Scene

Once you get to Nashville, the *Nashville Scene* will most likely be your new best friend, at least for a little while. Published each week, the magazine covers local politics, local restaurants, and the latest in music, arts, and entertainment. *Nashville Scene* has a wide distribution: It's everywhere, so don't be surprised if one walks up to you and introduces itself. The best part? It's free.

210 12th Ave. S.

Nashville, TN 37203

(615) 244-7989

www.nashvillescene.com

American Songwriter

This magazine speaks to the craft of songwriting across many genres. It delves into the technology of making recordings and reviews the latest gear and gadgets that are essential to a musician's tone. There are interviews with legendary artists, a lyric-writing contest, and record reviews.

American Songwriter

1303 16th Ave. S.

Nashville, TN 37212

(615) 321-6096

www.americansongwriter.com

Nashville Lifestyles

Once you get settled in Nashville this is a terrific magazine to have on the coffee table. It covers the movers and shakers in Nashville, culture, food and wine, and entertainment. The best issue, however, for musicians is the year-in-review music issue. It highlights musicians and singer-songwriters who have made some noise in the past year in Nashville.

1100 Broadway

Nashville, TN 37203

(615) 259-3636

www.nashvillelifestyles.com

CHAPTER 7
Road Trips

Land Between the Lakes.

O nce you're settled into your new life in Nashville networking, co-writing with another songwriter, and/or gigging out, you will come to a point where you'll want to leave the confines of the city and take in what Tennessee has to offer as a state. Memphis and Chattanooga are great places to go for a weekend getaway, but sometimes you don't want or can't afford to take off for a couple days. What you want is to hop in your car and spend some time either hiking, biking, or simply taking a long walk to clear your mind and be away from your day-to-day for a little while. I've often found that taking a long drive on a Saturday morning with my favorite tunes playing on the CD player in my car is an enjoyable way to take in the beauty of the Tennessee landscape. From downtown you can hit the road, and within a half hour at most you'll find yourself gliding through tree-lined valleys and thick woods. The ancient barns that dot the tranquil, expansive farmland still stand poetically, with their faded reddish colors and rusty barn door hinges symbolizing the passage of time.

In this chapter I've planned out four road trips that can easily be completed in one day. These trips are designed to either inspire a new song or to help you just get away from the hustle and bustle.

> **❝ There's nothing like music to relieve the soul and uplift it.❞**
> —Mickey Hart

Land Between the Lakes

Every time I head out to the Land Between the Lakes, or LBL, I pack a lunch, plenty of water, and a road map. The quickest way to get to LBL is to take I-24 west from Nashville heading in the direction of Kentucky. LBL is situated in both Tennessee and Kentucky. The Land Between the Lakes is so called because it is a strip of land that sits between Lake Barkley and Kentucky Lake. The southern entrance is on the Tennessee side and can be accessed by taking I-24 west until you reach Clarksville and pick up US 79 heading west toward Dover, Tennessee. This will put you at the bottom of LBL, and from there you'll want to head north. There is a welcome center that has maps and information for easy to difficult hiking or mountain bike trails. The only problem with taking this route is that US 79 can be slow going. Since this is meant to be a day trip, I'll offer up the best approach to making the most of your time in LBL.

Instead of getting off in Clarksville and picking up US 79, continue along I-24 West heading into Kentucky. After about twenty minutes or so, you'll want to exit at US 68/80 heading toward the town of Cadiz, Kentucky.

As far as I'm concerned, road trips and music go hand in hand, so for this outing I always take the Everly Brothers greatest hits. Sometimes music just makes the mood, and with songs like "Bowling Green" playing on the car stereo, the music and the landscape just seem to mesh. Once you get off the interstate, it will be another twenty-five minutes or so before you head over a bridge that spans Lake Barkley. It's a two-lane bridge and as alluring as the view can be, you need to focus on the road and the limited amount of space between you and the cars coming at you. This route will put you right in the middle of LBL, and your first stop should be the Golden Pond Visitor Center. The trip from Nashville to this portion of LBL will take you about an hour and a half. The visitor center has bathrooms and a gift shop, and offers a history of LBL along with a breakdown of all the wildlife that live there. There are also maps for those who want to take advantage of the walking trails located right near the visitors' center.

The biggest highlight for me has always been the Elk and Bison Prairie. You can buy a token to enter the prairie at the visitors' center for $5. Within minutes you will find yourself driving along a well-paved road staring at elk and bison that are grazing fifteen to twenty feet from the side of the road. It's best to stay in your car, but I have slowly gotten out of mine many times over the years to take photos. The remarkable thing is that the animals don't seem to mind. Just remember to put your car between you and the animals. I usually pull over to one of the rest areas in this loop and turn off the car. It never ceases to amaze me that a couple of hours from downtown Nashville, I'm sitting in a massive prairie watching these beautiful animals graze while having my own lunch. That's hard to match in other big cities around the country. The road in the prairie makes a natural loop, which leads to the exit, and from there you can hit the main road in LBL and either take a slow, leisurely drive down toward the bottom of LBL, which lets out by Dover, Tennessee, and US 79, or head back across the bridge that spans Lake Barkley and hit some of the rural roads in Kentucky.

If you decide to do the latter, I suggest you make the first right after you cross the bridge and pick up a two-lane country road, 164, toward Litton, Kentucky. The drive is very scenic, with old barns once used to dry tobacco painted red sitting by the side of the road. This route will eventually lead you back to I-24. Although it's not the quickest path, the drive is laid-back and tranquil. Because this is a small country road, be prepared to wave back at the other cars that pass you. It's a wonderful reminder that you're no longer in a big city and that you're driving through the beautiful farmland that makes up this part of southern Kentucky.

For more information:

Land Between the Lakes

(270) 924-2000

www.lbl.org

Music from underground. The Volcano Room, McMinnville, TN.

Bluegrass Underground at the Volcano Room

The other thing that never ceases to amaze me about Nashville—and Tennessee, for that matter—is that if there is a place where a musician or band can set up and play, Tennesseans will figure out a way to do it. The Volcano Room is no exception. WSM 650 AM radio hosts a monthly music series, broadcast from a cave 333 feet below the earth, called *Bluegrass Underground Live*. After you've made the trek down into the cave, you'll find a natural space that opens: It's there that bands perform. There are no elevators, so you have to walk the whole way down and back up. Along the way there are ancient stalactites hanging from the ceiling. The cave has to be one of the strangest places to see a live performance. If that weren't enough, there is a concession stand that sells food, hot coffee, candy bars, and sodas. There are restrooms, and for obvious reasons there is no alcohol allowed and smoking is prohibited. On the day I went, music enthusiasts of all ages made the fifteen-minute journey down into the Volcano Room. The ground can be moist and uneven, so wear a pair of sneakers or shoes with good grip. However, the female performer the day I went took the stage in a pair of boots with impossibly high heels. I was amazed and applauded her efforts to look sharp even this far underground. She was a pro and I thought to myself, "I guess the show must go on regardless where it takes place."

To get to the Volcano Room you'll have to take I-24 again, but this time heading east toward Manchester, Tennessee. From Nashville, it will take about an hour and a half to get to exit 111, McMinnville. Getting off the major interstates is a moment I look forward to, because once you get onto the country roads, you can kick back, relax, and take in the scenery. Take TN 55N to TN 287. After about five miles you'll come upon TN 108/127; this will lead you to TN 8, at which point look for signs that say "Cumberland Caverns." After a few miles on TN 8, you'll make a left onto Dark Hollow Road, which will lead you to Cumberland Caverns Road, which leads right up to the visitors' center, and there is plenty of parking, a restroom, and a gift shop.

If you're looking for a healthy lunch—say, a salad with almonds on top—this is not your place. So before you leave Nashville, pack a good lunch. I always take a couple of sandwiches, plenty of water, Gatorade, and some health bars. If I'm feeling especially festive, I pack some cheese and crackers for good measure.

The price of admission to the Volcano Room ranges, but for most shows it's $20. The cave can accommodate at least a hundred people, so small groups are led into the cave one group at a time an hour before the performance is scheduled to start. If you want to get a good seat, get there early and be part of the first group that goes down. Tickets can be bought online and will be waiting for you at will-call when you get to the visitors' center. If for some reason you don't want to stay for the whole performance, you can leave at any time and walk out of the cave on your own. The path is well lit and straightforward, so it's impossible to get lost. Shows start at 1:00 P.M. and last until 3:00 P.M. So if you leave Nashville at 10:00 A.M. and take in the show, you can be back in Nashville by 5:00 P.M. or so. The Volcano Room is at a constant 56 degrees, so packing a light jacket is a good idea. Finally, if you have a bat phobia, not to worry: I'm sure they're there, but I didn't see any. It's a well-known fact that bats are not fans of country or bluegrass, just goth.

For more information and tickets:

www.bluegrassunderground.com

Natchez Trace

This day trip is strictly for those of us who like driving. Sometimes I like going for a hike and other times I like to drive, listen to music, and sing along as the car does all the hard work transporting me through the landscape. The Natchez Trace is one of the most famous trails in this part of the country, and for centuries it was used as a trail between Nashville and Natchez, Mississippi. Today, the Trace is a two-lane country road that winds through farmland and forest alike in Middle Tennessee. The reason I've listed this as a day trip is because the speed limit along the trace is 50 mph, but most go slower than that. The one thing that you will notice right away is that there are no strip malls along the way. No McDonald's or commercial real estate, just natural scenery. There are plenty of opportunities along the Natchez Trace to pull over for a quick picnic or to get out of the car, walk around, and stretch your legs. You'll also want to make sure that your gas tank is full before you get to the Trace, for there are no gas stations here.

The best way to start this road trip is with a good meal. The Loveless Cafe, which I have mentioned throughout the book, is the perfect place to get a hearty southern breakfast complete with grits and some of the best homemade biscuits you'll ever find.

The easiest and most laid-back way to get to the Loveless Cafe is to pick up Highway 100 from West End in Nashville. The drive will take about thirty minutes, and the earlier you get to the Loveless, the better; the restaurant fills up quickly, and since we've got a road trip ahead of us, we don't want to waste time waiting for a table. After breakfast, you'll want to get back on Highway 100 and head south. That will lead you right into Natchez Trace. The one thing to keep in mind besides a full tank of gas is that the Trace runs for 444 miles. So what I do is check my watch after I've left the Loveless Cafe and clock it from there. Most of the time I'll get to where there is a monument dedicated to the explorer Meriwether Lewis, of Lewis and Clark fame. Once I reach that, I know it's probably a good time to head back to Nashville. As with most of the trips I've listed, if you leave Nashville around 9:00 A.M. or so, you can be back in time for an afternoon beer with your friends.

Radnor Lake

If you don't want to spend half the day in the car and you're just not up for a road trip, Radnor Lake is the perfect solution. Radnor Lake is at most twenty minutes from downtown Nashville, and although there are different ways to go, I like to pick up the 440 loop that goes around Nashville. This highway can be accessed by all of the interstates that pass through Nashville, including I-40, I-24, and I-65. Exit at Granny White Pike and then head south. The visitors' center is located at 1160 Otter Creek Road, off of Granny White Pike. There you can park and start your hike. The visitors' center has restrooms and maps for all the trails, which are well marked, so you can walk and get lost in your thoughts without getting lost. The trails range in difficulty, but most are easy; there are some trails that are marked "Strenuous," so if you're looking for an afternoon stroll through the woods or an early-morning weekend workout, you can do either and still have the rest of your day to write songs and take in a show later that night.

For more information:

www.radnorlake.org

(615) 251-1471

The General Jackson, Cumberland River, Nashville.

66 **Way down the river I hear a showboat band Big wheel a flashing, old _General Jackson_**99

—John Hartford, "General Jackson"

A Day Trip on the General Jackson

Out of all the day trips, this one is the least strenuous. An afternoon on the *General*, located on the banks of the Cumberland River out by Opry Mills Mall, might be just the thing to rejuvenate your soul. From downtown it's a twenty-minute drive, and because the General Jackson docks out by Opry Mills Mall there is plenty of parking. The entire cruise takes about two hours round trip. The *General* moves along the Cumberland at a leisurely pace to downtown Nashville's Riverfront Park and then heads back to Opry Mills.

On the top tier of the *General Jackson* is the hurricane deck, which is fitted with a lightweight blue-and-white awning to shade you from the sun, and an open floor plan for dancing. It's probably the last place you'd want to be during a hurricane, but rest assured, since Tennessee is landlocked, there is absolutely no threat of hurricanes—just tornados. The hurricane deck has two bars and a live band that plays country standards old and new. If you make good use of the "amenities" on the hurricane deck, I can almost guarantee that by the time you're about to dock back at port, you'll be singing "Sweet Home Alabama" at the top of your lungs with your shipmates.

The *General Jackson* offers two cruises a day, and serves up a buffet on its midday cruise and dinner on its evening cruise. The buffet and or dinner will cost a bit more, but if that's not in your game plan, you can just buy a ticket just for the hurricane deck and hang out with the other rowdies. I'd be remiss if I didn't mention the fact that the *General Jackson* is about three hundred feet long and sixty-five feet wide, leaving plenty of places, especially in the off-season, to sit back, relax, and watch the world go by at roughly six miles an hour.

From downtown, take I-40 east to exit 215, Briley Parkway 155 north. From there follow the signs that will take you to the Opry Mills Mall exit 11.

For more information about the *General Jackson* and cruise times:

General Jackson Showboat

2812 Opryland Dr.

Nashville, TN 37214

(615) 458-3900

www.generaljackson.com

CHAPTER 8
Nashville Breakdown: A Review

Home. Nashville, Tennessee.

66 Ninety-nine percent of the world's lovers are not with their first choice. That's what makes the jukebox play.99 —Willie Nelson

Nashville has an incredible history, and the music professionals that you will encounter, whether at the performance rights organizations; at a label; or a music publisher, all know Nashville's music history very well. You should too. Again, you don't need to know every nook and cranny of Nashville's music history, but I guarantee you will be a lot better off in the long run if you have a general sense of how Nashville became one of this country's most important music hubs.

Live

Finding a place to live and settling in will be a challenge, so I've made it easy by listing neighborhoods that musicians in Nashville seem to flock to. Making the move right away might not be the best plan of action. As many in this book have suggested, taking a trip to Nashville for a few days to get a sense of the city might be the way to go. If that's the case, try to plan that trip around one of Nashville's many music festivals and do yourself a favor: Contact the Nashville Chamber of Commerce as well as the visitors' center for more information before you leave. Both agencies are incredibly friendly and helpful.

If you haven't already done so, become a member of one of the PROs—ASCAP, BMI, or SESAC. If there is an NSAI chapter near you in your town or city, contact them as well and join. Once you get to Nashville, set up a meeting with the writer relations representatives at whichever PRO you have joined. Same goes for NSAI. Swing by their offices. They are located right off Music Row. Before you join, ask a lot of questions, take your time, and figure out if joining NSAI is right for you.

Make sure that you have a thorough understanding of the top music publishing terms that I listed in the "Musicians' Corner" chapter. Write a bio about yourself explaining what you're all about. Be passionate, and explain why it is you've taken to music/songwriting. Whatever you write, do not use the following words anywhere in your bio: "I was drawn to music at an early age." That line has been used to death, so avoid it at all costs.

Once you've done that, put together a package that contains your bio, a business card, and your CD. Be creative and make it engaging. Print out your song lyrics—maybe not all of them, but at least three to five of your best songs. On nice paper, please! And use a font that is readable. I've actually seen some lyric sheets with a tiny red font on purple paper. Useless. Make it easy for people to read and to get a quick understanding of who you are. Sometimes you might hear people say, "Give me the elevator pitch," about who you are and what you want to do with your music. Simply translated: "My time is limited: Give me the essence of who you are in the span of time that it takes an elevator to go from one floor to the next."

People want a story. Over the years, I've worked with many songwriters, and although it is all about the music, what I've tried to drive home to them is that people will listen to your song if you have an interesting story about yourself. If you hear an interview with a songwriter on the radio and you're drawn to that person because of what they say, you're more willing to give their music a chance. Make sense?

Music, in its truest form, is a connection, and it's a shared process between you, the songwriter, and the listener. Therefore, you should think about your favorite bands or songwriters, make a list of what it is about them and their songs that makes you connect. Use a lot of adjectives when you write this down. This will give you and everyone you're dealing with in Nashville a better sense of who you are and what you're trying to do with your music.

Network

As has been suggested throughout the book you need to get out and network. The best place to do this is at the open mic/writers' nights. All of the venues that I've mentioned in this book are great places to network, so try and hit a couple during the week and just listen.

Don't bring your guitar. Just sit back and get a sense of the vibe. If you're a drummer, bass player, or saxophone player, these venues are great for meeting other musicians and potentially to get a band started. Once you feel that you've done your homework and scouted out some of the open mic/writers' nights around town, it's time to play one. The key thing to remember is that Nashville and Nashville musicians are humble, so don't be a show-off, or be a know-it-all. Let your music do the talking for you.

Be supportive of others and they will be supportive of you, or, as another saying goes, "You get what you give."

Succeed

When you decide that you're ready to play an open mic night, think about how you're going to introduce the songs that you will play that night. Make it engaging, and whatever you do, don't make the introduction longer than the song itself. Again, this is a big no-no, and yet it happens all the time. The more precise, heartfelt, and articulate you are in introducing your song, the more people will want to listen.

When you start making connections and meeting music industry professionals and music publishers, remember that you are in business for yourself. You are in control. If you have a meeting of importance down on Music Row, show up fifteen minutes early and listen to what that person has to say. Whether it's a music publishing company, record label, or whatever, Google it and read about the company's history. It will most likely not come up in conversation, but it is for your own good, because, as we all know, information is key. After the meeting, follow up with a quick thank-you note and drop it in the mail that day. E-mail is fine as well, but nothing says that you really care and appreciated that person's time like a handwritten note.

Make Your Scene

Finally, you're in Nashville to create a life where music is a big part of your every day. Luckily, Nashville makes that easy. The friendships you make, the music you record, and the experience of establishing yourself in Nashville can, in itself, be considered a crowning achievement. You've already taken the first and most important step, which is following your passion for music. Personally, I can't think of any better pursuit than that. Keep your eyes and ears open, embrace all that Nashville has to offer, and I'll see you at the Ryman.

BIBLIOGRAPHY

Country Music Hall of Fame and Museum, compiler. 2004. *The Encyclopedia of Country Music: The Ultimate Guide to the Music.* Edited by Paul Kingsbury. New York: Oxford University Press.

Havighurst, Craig. 2007. *Air Castle of the South: WSM and the Making of Music City.* Urbana: University of Illinois Press.

Kosser, Michael. 2006. *How Nashville Became Music City, U.S.A.: 50 Years of Music Row.* New York: Hal Leonard.

McDaniel, Karina. 2005. *Nashville Then and Now.* San Diego, CA: Thunder Bay Press.

Oermann, Robert K. 2008. *Behind the Grand Ole Opry Curtain: Tales of Romance and Tragedy.* New York: Center Street.

Pugh, Ronnie. 1998. *Ernest Tubb: The Texas Troubadour.* Durham, NC: Duke University Press.

Wolfe, Charles K. 1999. *A Good-Natured Riot: The Birth of the Grand Ole Opry.* Nashville, TN: Vanderbilt University Press / Country Music Foundation Press.

Zepp, George R. 2009. *Hidden History of Nashville.* Charleston, SC: The History Press.

Zwonitzer, Mark, and Charles Hirshberg. 2004. *Will You Miss Me When I'm Gone: The Carter Family and Their Legacy in American Music.* New York: Simon & Schuster.

Other Resources:

Ryman Auditorium Backstage Tour
116 Fifth Ave. N.
Nashville, TN 37219
(615) 889-3060

Country Music Hall of Fame and Museum
222 Fifth Ave. S.
Nashville, TN 37203
(615) 416-2001

Websites:

www.roughstock.com

INDEX